✦ **BLACK CORPORATE EXECUTIVES**

In the series *Labor and Social Change,*
edited by Paula Rayman and Carmen Sirianni

BLACK CORPORATE EXECUTIVES ✦

The Making and Breaking of a Black Middle Class

Sharon M. Collins

Temple University Press ✦ *Philadelphia*

305.896073
C71b

Temple University Press, Philadelphia 19122
Copyright © 1997 by Sharon M. Collins. All rights reserved
Published 1997
Printed in the United States of America

∞ The paper used in this book meets the requirements of the American National Standard for Information Sciences — Permanence of Paper for Printed Library Materials, ANSI Z39.48-1984

Text design by Nighthawk Design

Library of Congress Cataloging-in-Publication Data

Collins, Sharon M., 1947–
    Black corporate executives : the making and breaking of a black middle class / Sharon M. Collins.
        p.   cm. — (Labor and social change)
    Includes bibliographical references and index.
    ISBN 1-56639-473-2 (cloth : alk. paper). — ISBN 1-56639-474-0 (pbk. : alk. paper)
        1. Afro-American executives — Illinois — Chicago — Case studies. 2. Afro-Americans — Employment — Case studies. 3. Discrimination in employment — United States — Case studies.   I. Title.   II. Series.
HD38.25.U6C65   1996
305.8'96073 — dc20   96-10735

To Annie, Fernie, Robyn, and Michael
and in memory of Fernando Collins, my father,
and Sheila Groot, my sister

CONTENTS

TABLES AND FIGURES

Tables

Figures

PREFACE

✦ The idea for this project arose in 1980 as I started to contemplate the relationship between economic opportunities for middle-class African Americans and federal government policies and legislation. This contemplation was triggered, in part, by emergent national attitudes that viewed race-based programs as ineffective — even harmful — for impoverished blacks and affirmative-action programs as unnecessary favoritism bestowed on a black middle class that could well compete without them. These attitudes congealed around Ronald Reagan's election to the White House and his campaign promise to cut back government bureaucracy, particularly social welfare programs that proliferated during the 1960s War on Poverty. Moreover, the Reagan White House openly challenged the policy and practice of affirmative action — a policy that in the previous decade had symbolized victory in the war on race-based employment discrimination.

William Wilson's 1978 book *The Declining Significance of Race* reflected some of these attitudes, through its title if not entirely its substance. A 1980 article by Carl Gershman and Kenneth Clark in the *New York Times* reflected these attitudes as well, articulating two sides of the debate on whether class or race effects blacks' economic opportunities. Increasingly, it seemed to me, editorials and new black spokespeople were stepping up to accuse traditional black civil rights leadership of exploiting the poor and manipulating federal policies and racial problems to gain narrow and self-serving resolutions.

But a more personal ingredient also provoked the idea for this project: my introduction to a new social stratum that included the black business elite of Chicago. This group of successful and well-known executives worked in high-paying jobs in Chicago's major corporations or were entrepreneurs who owned the largest — and possibly the only — black-owned company of its type in the nation. These people also integrated major companies during the mid-1960s and early 1970s when higher-paying jobs became accessible to blacks in the midst of civil rights upheaval.

The life-styles I observed appeared solidly upper middle class, even affluent, the executives imbued with conspicuous social privileges that flowed from their unique status. Yet, as these black businesspeople conferred among themselves about what they perceived to be the beginning of a new era of entrenchment in race relations, their tones conveyed fear. Although solidly assimilated into the social and economic mainstream of a major U.S. city, they feared the new public discourse and a federal agenda that threatened to dismantle the race-based programs that had assisted their rise.

Ultimately, then, this project was the culmination of my search to answer the question, What were these talented, educated, and economically successful people afraid of? (If William Wilson and others were right — if indeed class is more salient than race in predicting blacks' chances in the labor market — the changes in national policy should have little, if any, effect on them.) What I saw during this period, and in my own career trajectory, suggested to me a theory about blacks' job opportunity structure since the mid-1960s. I believe that race was a status that changed, albeit temporarily, from negative to positive during this period. This new positive status enabled some blacks to experience rapid upward economic mobility.

My theory evolved into an answer to my initial question. Although the people I observed were affluent, the system of jobs that supported their life-styles was a product of a particular historical period in which the federal government made efforts to improve the status of blacks. As federal policies and programs oriented toward blacks multiplied during the 1960s and 1970s, the number of professional and administrative jobs available to the black middle class multiplied dramatically. In 1980, however, the Reagan presidency, and its powerful challenge to the antibias legislation and welfare policies of the previous fifteen years, demonstrated that this period was ending. Black civil rights upheaval abated and, not coincidentally, so did federal expenditures and supports that created black economic opportunities. In short, when the government's approach to welfare expenditures and antibias policy altered, the economic base that enabled these people to rise economically and socially and to maintain their new life-styles was directly threatened.

A popular view among scholars and public policymakers is that macroeconomic and demographic trends stimulated growth in the African American middle class. I argue, however, that since the 1960s the African American middle class grew in a labor market in which government policy and intervention created job opportunities. The African American middle class is therefore a politically mediated, not a market-mediated, creature. In my view, job opportunities for middle-class blacks were enhanced by jobs, roles, and institutions created and expanded to alleviate black discontent and the social upheaval of the 1960s. Central to this thesis is the notion that the political foundations supporting blacks' class advancement puts the progress of African Americans in double jeopardy. The threat of downward mobility for African Americans in the middle class comes from changes both in the public-policy agenda and in the economy.

ACKNOWLEDGMENTS

✦ I have benefited from so much encouragement and advice that to thank each person by name I would need an acknowledgment as long as the manuscript itself. Therefore, I will say only that I appreciate each individual and have thanked every one of them in my private moments and, in many cases, in public as well.

There are people, however, to whom I owe a particularly large debt: My husband — one of the black businesspeople I refer to in the preface — and Dr. Arnold Feldman are among them. At the very outset, both helped me to articulate and formulate my ideas and to give them substance and logic. Arnold Feldman did this in his role as my professor at Northwestern University, while offering his unfailing dedication as my first full-fledged intellectual mentor. James Lowry, my husband, helped guide me with the perceptiveness of someone who well understood that his adult life was shaped in large part by the forces discussed in this book. Near the end of this project, Mildred Schwartz and John Johnstone — my colleagues at the University of Illinois, Chicago — stood by me, read my work, and cheered me on when I needed, but was unable to request, the structure and encouragement to complete it. To these people, and to all the others who helped to shape the ideas in this book, I offer my thanks.

✦ **BLACK CORPORATE EXECUTIVES**

Chapter 1

The Controversy over Race and Class

✦ Since at least the 1960s, the federal government has attempted to improve the economic and social status of blacks with legislation and policies to enhance and protect blacks' employment, voting, and housing rights. One result of government legislation, particularly laws designed to eradicate employment discrimination, was to allow significant numbers of skilled and college-educated blacks to enter the middle class through higher-paying professional and managerial jobs. Thus, blacks whose training and education positioned them to take advantage of federally mandated hiring practices began to compete in mainstream avenues to economic success and well-being (Farley 1984; Freeman 1976a). However, despite government intervention, the social and economic problems of many already disadvantaged blacks multiplied dramatically during the same period (Jaynes and Williams 1989).

Stark contrasts between the socioeconomic progress of contemporary blacks in the middle class and deteriorating conditions in the ghetto raise questions about what influences economic opportunities for black Americans. Researchers ask whether a new system of stratification in the labor market is evolving that responds to attributes associated more with class than with race. Here I take a different path to exploring the relationship between class and race by examining the role of political pressure and the careers of blacks in white corporate management.

I concentrate on relatively privileged blacks because my analysis of labor market trends since the 1960s demonstrates that characteristics associated with black advancement differ from those highlighted in existing research using aggregate data. In light of this analysis, I evaluate other research perspectives that perceive class, education, and skills, not race, as the deciding factors in the black experience. I also examine what those research perspectives imply for public policy.

The labor market analysis underpins an alternative paradigm that becomes the basis for interpreting the research presented here. In this paradigm, the middle class that sprang up among blacks benefiting from the civil rights movement is viewed as a politically mediated class, in this case, a class dependent on collective black protest, the growth of federal social programs and expenditures, and governmental antibias policy and intervention. Occupational gains made within the black middle class since the 1960s are fragile. Since the 1980s, these gains have been threatened as much by political changes in the African American community and by changes in federal policy as by macroeconomic trends.

Living the American Dream

Federal legislation to protect black citizenship rights, such as the Civil Rights Act of 1964, the Voting Rights Act of 1965, and Title VIII in the Civil Rights Act of 1968 (on housing), raised hopes that exclusionary systems that targeted blacks would erode. During the 1960s these hopes began to be realized in the labor market as employment practices changed and blacks' pattern of little or no occupational progress relative to whites finally altered. Before the 1960s, blacks' rate of entry into higher-paying occupations and white-collar jobs lagged far behind whites' and showed minimal progress. Except for periods of severe labor shortage during the two world wars, blacks' economic standing was severely limited by racial prejudice and may have even deteriorated during the Great Depression (Freeman 1976; Newman et al. 1978). Employment discrimination in the South restricted blacks primarily to field jobs in agriculture and to subservient positions, such as maids and cooks in private households. Even in the North, blacks were cast as inferior workers, excluded from lucrative industries and establishments and from jobs white workers found attractive. However, the enactment of modern civil rights legislation, in particular the Civil Rights Act of 1964, signaled a dramatic shift in blacks' ability to compete in the marketplace. Data for the 1960s and 1970s show marked increases in black-white male earning ratios (Smith and Welch 1977, 1978a; 1978b) and in the proportions of blacks in the professions (Freeman 1976a, 1976b, 1981). Moreover, occupational distributions for employed black men began to approximate those for employed white men (Farley 1977; Featherman and Hauser 1976; Hauser and Featherman 1974).

Advances in the African American Middle Class

Both E. Franklin Frazier (1957) and William Wilson (1978) define the black middle class in economic terms: blacks employed in white-collar, craftsmen, and foremen positions. By this definition, during the period of federal civil rights activity and the expansion of domestic assistance programs, blacks moved steadily into the U.S. middle class, joining the economic mainstream.

Between 1960 and 1980, blacks entered white-collar jobs at a rate much faster than did whites. The proportion of blacks in white-collar jobs increased 80 percent between 1960 and 1970, and 44 percent more between 1970 and 1979 (Figures 1 and 2). Overall, blacks more than doubled their proportion in white-collar jobs. By 1980, the proportion of blacks in white-collar jobs had increased a total of 124 percent, compared to only 25 percent for whites. At the other end of the occupational pyramid, the proportion of blacks in blue-collar jobs remained relatively constant, while the proportions in service and farm jobs declined sharply.

Blacks' upward mobility looked vastly different for men and women. African American women shifted from domestic and personal-service jobs into clerical and sales positions, but black men

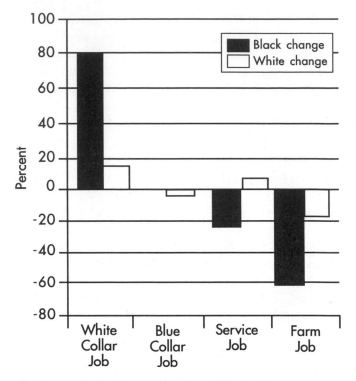

Figure 1. Changes in Employment by Race: 1960–1970

moved into professional jobs, including management and business-oriented professions such as accounting and law, for the first time in U.S. history. Thus, during the decades in which black initiatives set precedent for public policy, the occupational gap between skilled and highly educated black and white men began to shrink, although disparities remained (Featherman and Hauser 1976; Freeman 1976a; Smith and Welch 1977).

In 1960, only 5 percent of employed black men worked in better-paying white-collar occupations; by 1979, 11 percent did. Between 1960 and 1979, the proportion of black men in professional, technical, and managerial fields more than doubled. In contrast, the proportion of white men in the same fields increased only 18 percent (U.S. Bureau of the Census 1979, 1980). Although the economic

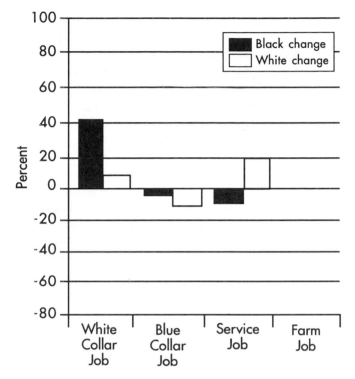

Figure 2. Changes in Employment by Race: 1970–1980

position of blacks still lags far behind that of whites, blacks — especially skilled or highly educated workers — have experienced substantial economic gains since the 1960s.

Deterioration in the Underclass

But as skilled and highly educated blacks reaped gains from civil rights protest and subsequent federal policies, the social and economic problems of the black underclass remained intransigent.[1] Life for blacks in inner-city ghettos became worse, not better, following the 1960s civil rights efforts. One in three blacks live below the poverty line, and blacks are about three times as likely as whites to be poor. Moreover, from the 1970s through the mid-1980s, the absolute and relative probability that blacks will be impoverished remained almost unchanged despite decades of governmental intervention to improve their socioeconomic status. Blacks with relatively less work experience and black female-headed households have fallen behind the general population during more than a decade of affirmative action and federal domestic assistance programs (Becker and Hills 1979; Freeman 1973; Mare and Winship 1980; Ross and Sawhill 1975).

The proportion of blacks who live below the poverty line, who are unemployed, or who have dropped out of the labor force remains discouragingly high (Farley and Bianchi 1983; Glasgow 1980; Ismail 1985; Parsons 1980). In short, economic conditions for unskilled blacks and blacks with low levels of education deteriorated at the same time economic opportunities for middle-class blacks flourished.

Perspectives on Black Economic Attainment

The bifurcated trends in blacks' access to labor markets have generated a heated debate on blacks' competitiveness in the U.S. economy (see Gershman and Clark 1980). Scholars such as Feagin and Sikes (1994), Zweigenhaft and Domhoff (1991), and Landry (1987) maintain that discrimination remains an obstacle to blacks' full economic participation, that institutional practices and individual prejudice erect barriers that still restrict blacks' economic chances, regardless of education, skills, and other class-related advantages. However, others argue convincingly that blacks' economic chances more likely are mediated by "nonracial" factors associated with class—family background and schooling—than by racial discrimination. For instance, Smith and Welch (1983, 1986) found that improvements in blacks' occupational status coincided with improvements in the quantity and quality of black education. Such findings tend to minimize the weight of race-based obstacles that restrict blacks' access to labor-market opportunities. Their underlying assumption is that race discrimination is more an individual anomaly or aberration than an entrenched characteristic of U.S. society. Other research connects disparity in occupational mobility to age and regional differences between black and white populations (Featherman and Hauser 1976; Hout 1984). Since education, region, and age are examples of "nonracial" explanations of blacks' differential attainment, such findings corroborate the claim that job opportunities for blacks are not anchored to racial discrimination, per se.

The Role of Economic Structure and Culture

The idea that racial barriers are eroding presumes that as blacks in the middle class attain quality educations and ascend occupational ladders, they assimilate into the economic mainstream. At the same time, barriers to black employment other than race — such as culture and macroeconomic changes — are seen to confront the underclass (Becker 1981, chap. 11; Murray 1984; Wilson 1978, 1987). For example, individuals who drop out, or are pushed out, of labor markets due to social pathology (Wilson 1987) and welfare incentives (Becker 1981; Murray 1984) are evidence of cultural deficits within inner-city black communities. More female-headed households and dependence on government welfare programs, along with reduced labor-force participation among adult black men, also illustrate dysfunctional ghetto features. These observations are not new. But unlike earlier theorists that portray dysfunctional ghetto features as a response to, not separate from, the conditions of the greater society, recent critics of inner-city culture argue that economic deterioration among blacks results from the self-imposed constraints of social disorganization and undeveloped human resources. This portrait of social disorganization among the black poor contrasts sharply with those of theorists — Kenneth Clark (1965), in particular — who linked ghetto pathology to racial prejudice and the pervasive structure of racial inequality. The current argument is that the dysfunctional components of ghetto life are no longer a symptom of contemporary racial discrimination and subordination (see Wilson 1987).

Even structural explanations for the massive deterioration of inner-city life dismiss racial discrimination as a background factor. A structural perspective attributes the plight of blacks in poor urban areas primarily to massive changes in the postindustrial economy (e.g. Harrington 1984; Wilson 1987). Wilson (1987) follows the lead of Kasarda (1980; 1986), for example, and views economic deterioration among blacks as an outgrowth of deindustrialization. Both scholars argue that rapid changes in urban industrial bases displace minority workers by creating a mismatch in which minority residents' educational backgrounds are no longer compatible with the incoming industries' needs. During the heyday of heavy industry, employment levels among blacks were high, especially in urban centers where blue-collar blacks found low-skilled but relatively high-wage jobs in industries like auto and steel manufacturing. But smokestack industries declined, and urban employment shifted into fast-growing service industries in which wages are polarized. Historically, blacks have been underrepresented in high-wage jobs in service industries. Conversely, low-skilled and blue-collar black workers have been concentrated disproportionately in poor-paying service jobs or quickly evaporating jobs in urban industries (Wilson 1987). In sum, the shift from goods- to service-producing industries and the accompanying decline in wages — rather than race per se — have dislocated black workers.

In this picture, scholars constructed a paradigm in which race is understood to play a diminished role in black employment relative to cultural and structural factors, which are seen increasingly to restrict opportunities available to less-advantaged blacks. Simultaneously, cultural and structural factors — in the form of valued education and skills and the expansion of skilled and high-paying jobs in service industries — benefit better-educated blacks in the middle class. Put another way, the same macroeconomic trends that cast working-class blacks into the underclass (e.g., shifts in technology and the increased numbers of white-collar jobs generated by service industries) also created new and better opportunities for other blacks to enter the middle class. In this scenario, dual forces converged to erode longstanding racial barriers to blacks with skills: the increased need for skilled workers brought on by an expanding service economy, on one hand, and educational improvements in the supply of black labor, on the other.

Structural and cultural perspectives, then, see the structure of occupations becoming increasingly color-blind. Not racial discrimination but black social dysfunction fed by welfare dependence, family background, and limited job skills explains race-related job inequality and low status. Conversely, the increased acquisition of marketable work skills and quality education for blacks already higher on the occupational ladder explains that segment's ascent to the middle class and emerging ability to successfully compete with whites.

Public-Policy Implications

The controversy over which factors influence economic opportunities for black Americans is not a theoretical exercise limited to academic arenas. The question also has public policy implications because the opposing ideologies justify divergent strategies for solving blacks' economic problems. In the 1960s, a politically liberal view that justified governmental protection and race-based policy as critical to black advancement prevailed among black intellectuals and leaders. However, since the 1980s, more conservative, essentially nonracial explanations of blacks' status in the economy have justified dismantling race-specific programs. For example, Wilson (1987), Glenn Loury (1985), Thomas Sowell (1983), and Carl Gershman (Gershman and Clark 1980) have argued that many contemporary problems of blacks fail to respond to race-based governmental interventions. Moreover, they argue, liberalism, black activism, and misguided government actions have fostered, rather than ameliorated, such problems. Wilson (1987), in particular, holds that two decades of race-based employment policy created opportunities for advantaged blacks but neglected to address training-based barriers to employment faced by disadvantaged blacks. In other words, the race-specific agenda tied to programs such as affirmative action created access to previously closed jobs, but only for those blacks who had the skills and education to compete for them.

Gershman (Gershman and Clark 1980), Loury (1985), and Wilson (1981) issue even more severe indictments of the political agenda they perceive as underpinning civil rights–related social policy. These authors paint black intellectuals and political leaders as self-serving advocates of race-specific government programs that are ill-suited to the needs of the poor. In their view, the liberalism of black leadership has led to remedial employment policies and programs that were exploited to gain jobs for advantaged blacks. Gershman and Loury also contend that governmental welfare programs, such as public assistance stipends, subsidized goods and services that fostered dependency among underclass blacks (also see Murray 1984; Sowell 1983; Williams 1982). In sum, race-specific programs and policies that have evolved since the 1960s have been under attack since the 1980s. In the 1990s, their role is challenged and their future remains in question. However, the growing consensus is that color-blind labor markets, not race-conscious policies, will protect and sustain black gains in jobs formerly closed to them.

A Different Paradigm of Race and Class

I differ with those who argue that blacks' gains in higher-paying jobs provide evidence that economic opportunities for blacks are linked to culture, education, and skills, not racial characteristics. I begin instead with the assumption that race remains important, even for the black middle class. However, I do not recapitulate earlier arguments that directly linked racial discrimination with blocked economic attainment. I believe that economic advances by the black middle class since the 1960s civil rights movement are considerable. At the same time, I view the black middle class of professional and managerial workers as a politically mediated class that fills a socially useful function. This class plays a unique role in the labor market and occupies a fragile position.

I also differ from researchers who take a narrow view of the effects of federal legislation on employment and depict equal opportunity employment legislation as the government's only method for spurring upward mobility among blacks. Such a narrow focus on regulatory policies obscures the indirect employment effects of government advocacy.[2] These indirect employment effects are job opportunities generated by an expanding network of government and private sector bureaucracy to increase the distribution of goods and services to volatile black constituencies. I view the black middle class as resulting both from public policy supports — such as federal legislation prohibiting employment discrimination, and the growth in federal social service bureaucracy — and from jobs created or reoriented to respond to blacks' civil rights–related demands and upheaval.

My conception of the black middle class is uncoupled from occupational categories. Rather, I define it by its relationship to a system of production. I hold that one by-product of race-conscious policies and programs was a new employment structure from which educated middle-class blacks have benefited. I suggest that better jobs for blacks may not be merely a factor of education or even the effect of affirmative action. Better jobs may depend also on substantive changes in the organization of jobs, a result of the need felt by the federal government and private employers to abate black upheaval and restore social order, which had been disrupted by civil rights activities.

Specifically, demands for black-oriented programs and employment policies altered the organization of jobs and institutions to distribute more services and financial resources to blacks. During the 1960s and 1970s, administrative functions and race-specific programs were created, expanded, or reinterpreted to respond to blacks' needs, which also increased the number of professional and administrative jobs available to middle-class blacks. More significantly, opportunities for good jobs in white-dominated settings emerged in a black-oriented delivery system. Blacks, therefore, remained "functionally segregated" in the labor market; black professionals in white institutions filled roles tied to the appeasement of blacks. They were not hired or promoted to meet the demands of total (predominantly white) constituencies. Executives I studied played a socially useful role in white companies during the 1960s and 1970s, but by the 1980s, they had become economically expendable.

In Chapter 3, I present evidence of functional segregation of blacks, showing first that during the 1970s, higher-paying jobs for blacks in the public sector were differentially concentrated in urban bureaucracies that serve disproportionately large concentrations of blacks. When federal funding expanded urban services targeting blacks, middle-class blacks were tracked into jobs that were developed to allocate additional resources to impoverished blacks and to restore social order. I also present evidence of functional segregation in private sector employment. For example, during the 1970s the first black-owned advertising agency was founded in Chicago. This agency was hired by white companies to reach out to black (but not white) consumer markets. Further, reorganization of work into racialized roles added a ghettoized component to blacks' gains in management during the 1960s and 1970s. Blacks were disproportionately moved into personnel departments and labor- and public-relations jobs (U.S. Bureau of the Census 1963, 1973) to administer corporate policies sensitive to blacks and, hence, lessen racial pressures on white corporate environments.

In this conception of how the black middle class grew during the 1960s and 1970s, even if the black middle class — more than the underclass — benefited economically from political demands, the benefits are mediated by blacks' political dependency. And, since the federal government and private employers do not respond to the black population unless it is disruptive, when pressures abate organizations will cut back race-conscious services and thereby dislocate people who became middle class by performing them. In this conception, the black middle class is the interim beneficiary of social policy to ameliorate black upheaval. The long-term beneficiaries are the larger systems of white elites.

The Investigation

To test my ideas about the labor market for blacks, I conducted two sets of in-depth interviews with the seventy-six highest-ranking black executives in Fortune 500 companies — the people whom researchers, public policy makers, and the general public refer to when they talk about black breakthroughs. I conducted the first interviews in 1986, the second in 1992. Conformity to corporate cultures, personal networks, and skill are key factors in individual mobility among high-ranking executives. Therefore, if any blacks can be said to have transcended racial barriers, it would be these executives. They are the ultimate black middle-class beneficiaries of the civil rights movement.

I considered blacks to be "top executives" if: (1) they were employed in a banking institution and held the title of comptroller, trust officer, vice-president (excluding "assistant" vice-president), president, or chief officer; or (2) they were employed in a nonfinancial institution and held the title of department manager, director, vice-president, or chief officer. I located these executives by using *Chicago Reporter* (1983; 1986) lists that cite the fifty-two largest white-owned industrials, utilities, retail companies, transportation companies, and banks in Chicago. I then asked knowledgeable persons familiar with the white corporate community in Chicago to identify black officers in these firms and other employees who might be able to provide names of higher-level black officers. I then asked these employees to identify blacks at the selected levels of management. Finally, I asked black executives who participated in the study to identify other top blacks in the selected Chicago firms. Eighty-seven executives were identified; seventy-six were interviewed.[3] Executive headhunters and business executives confirmed that I had defined and located nearly the entire population of senior level black executives employed in Chicago.

Although it is difficult to specify the exact number of blacks who met the study criteria, publications that feature the nation's top-ranking black executives, such as *Dollars and Sense* and *Black Enterprise,* routinely mention the people I interviewed.

In the mid-1980s, the interviewees held some of the more desirable and prestigious positions in Chicago corporations. Contrary to a popular notion that black women are greater beneficiaries of affirmative action than black men—in part because they fall into two federally regulated categories—only thirteen of the seventy-six executives were women. The joint effects of race and sex discrimination made black women largely absent in the higher-paying ranks of management and, indeed, the last to benefit from federal affirmative-action legislation (Leonard 1988).

Almost two-thirds of the men and half the women held the title of director or above, including three chief officers, thirty vice-presidents, and nineteen unit directors. (The total includes three people with the title "manager" whose rank within the organization was equivalent to director.) In addition to being the top people in Chicago in 1986, some of the interviewees were among the highest-ranking black executives in the country. Five of the men were the highest-ranking blacks in corporations nationwide. Almost half (thirty-two of seventy-six) were the highest-ranking blacks in their companies' nationwide management structure.

In the 1986 interviews, I explored whether or not these executives filled racialized roles that had emerged during the racially tumultuous civil rights period. Using resumés they had sent me before the formal interview, I conducted semistructured interviews in which I asked the executives to describe in detail each job they had held over the course of their careers. When a manager's description of a job or the nature of a job was unclear, or when it was not feasible to examine careers on a job-by-job basis, I asked, "During the late 1960s and early 1970s, social programs such as EEO [equal employment opportunity], manpower training, and community affairs were hot items in some corporations. Did you ever have a job in any of these areas?" Using their answers I differentiated the "racialized" and "mainstream" tasks for each job held by a manager. I considered jobs racialized if their description suggested a substantive or a symbolic connection to black communities, black issues, or civil rights agencies at any level of government. For example, one manager was hired by a major retailer in 1968 specifically to discover and eliminate discriminatory employment practices. I coded this function "racialized" since it was designed to improve blacks' opportunities within the company at a time when the federal government increasingly was requiring such revisions. I labeled jobs "mainstream" if their descriptions revealed neither explicit nor implicit connections to blacks.

Fifty-one of these executives (67 percent) had held one or more jobs in a company in which they implemented corporate programs for, funneled corporate goods and services to, or advised the white corporate elite about black constituents. In both 1986 and 1992, I explored the possibility that racialized management positions lack job security because the need for racialized functions would vary in tandem with political conditions. I began my interviews with the hypothesis that since racialized jobs emerged in response to political pressures, they are likely to be treated as increasingly expendable as that pressure subsides. Between 1992 and 1994 I located and reinterviewed sixty-one of the original seventy-six executives to capture how they had fared under rapidly changing economic and political conditions.[4] (I also talked with people in the business world familiar both with Chicago's corporate executives and with various internal events not likely to be known outside the business community. They kept me up to date on Chicago's business news and helped me interpret events that had implications for the study.) These follow-up interviews provided a second and stronger test of my argument.

In Chapters 2 and 3, I show that black mobility within the middle class during the 1960s and 1970s was politically mediated, that black social protest and federal government intervention expanded job opportunities for middle-class blacks during that period. I show how this politically mediated system of economic mobility produced a race-based job inequality that contributes to black middle-class fragility, particularly from the 1980s onward.

The remainder of the book draws on the interviews I conducted in 1986 and 1992. In Chapter 4 I look at the social and political conditions surrounding the entry of this successful cohort of black managers into major white corporations. In Chapters 5 and 6, I consider blacks' roles inside white corporations and review how and why these executives stayed in black-related jobs. Chapters 7 and 8 include the executives' perceptions of their own status changes within their companies. The story unfolds amidst a history that began with the expanding economy and race-conscious pressures of the 1960s and evolved into the increased economic and interest-group competition of the 1990s.

Some readers may be tempted to view this book as an indictment of race-based policies; that would be a misinterpretation. The people in this study are the most privileged, the ultimate beneficiaries of changes wrought by the civil rights movement. Having "made it" by almost any socioeconomic standard, they represent evidence that race-based policies have facilitated upward mobility for some segments of the black population. However, my intent here is to illustrate the resilience of segregating systems, even under social conditions designed to improve race relations. Public policy did indeed help some blacks grasp the American dream. Yet, now, twenty-five years later, many have hit the race-specific glass ceiling endemic to racialized roles. The same conditions that helped blacks succeed in corporate hierarchies also channeled them out of mainstream job functions and locked them into limited and fragile career paths.

Chapter 2

A Politically Mediated Opportunity Structure

✦ Affirmative action has come under siege recently not only as a politically unpopular program but as an ineffective policy for reducing inequality for targeted groups.[1] However, attempts to minimize and devalue the federal government's role in the upward mobility of blacks have not been decisive. Studies find that affirmative action and contract compliance significantly improved employment opportunities for blacks (Heckman and Payner 1989; Herring and Collins 1995; Leonard 1982). In addition, researchers who argue that federal intervention played a trivial role in blacks' mobility fail to consider the effects of employment opportunities that sprang directly from the proliferation of federally funded welfare and community-service organizations that coincided with blacks' protest for civil rights. (Civil rights activity in the 1960s only stimulated federal government efforts already underway on behalf of blacks; the first equal employment laws were established in the 1940s.)

Before the 1960s, women and people of color were the victims of employment discrimination (Burstein 1985; Farley 1984; Farley and Allen 1987; Jaynes and Williams 1989; Wilson 1978). In the effort to curtail such discrimination, since at least the 1940s executive orders have been issued and federal legislation enacted to prohibit discrimination against minorities and women workers.[2]

In the early 1940s, President Roosevelt issued executive orders declaring an end to discrimination in the federal civil service and cr ating the Fair Employment Practices Committee. The federal effort to prohibit discrimination continued during the 1950s when President Truman issued two executive orders to establish fair employment procedures within the federal government structure, to abolish discrimination in the armed forces, and to establish compliance procedures for government contractors. Given the entrenched nature of discriminatory employment patterns on the one hand and the escalation of black protest on the other, it is not surprising that the Civil Rights Act of 1964 was passed to further propel this legislative process.

While a variety of employment situations exist within the black middle class, patterns of blacks' upward mobility in the 1960s and 1970s were clearly not just the product of blacks' accumulation of skill and training. Members of the black middle class benefited from participating in labor markets shaped during the 1960s and 1970s in response to blacks' civil rights demands and the ensuing federal legislation. "Although blacks in the U.S. were better off absolutely in the 1960s than ever before in American history, their sense of deprivation relative to whites proved explosive" (Blumberg 1980). The demands of African Americans for greater investment in community and economic development, articulated by black leadership, set the ground rules for a social policy during the administrations of Kennedy, Johnson, and Nixon that generated growth in federal legislation and spending, inflating the labor market for blacks in both the public and private sectors. This inflation was the result of new bureaucracies and the enforcing of affirmative-action guidelines tied to federal expenditures.

Production's demand for labor can be conceptualized as an economic or policy response to consumers. Economic mandates are a response to consumer preferences mediated in the market. Policy mandates are a response to political pressure mediated through government. In the case of affirmative action, government enhanced the status of blacks by establishing employers' need for them, which in turn expanded labor-market demand. Employers sought college-educated blacks to fill higher-paying white-collar jobs, which translated into opportunities for new class position. Therefore, the black middle class that emerged during the 1960s and 1970s is a result of a policy-mediated, not a market-mediated, situation. This paradigm is meant not to rigidly characterize how the black middle class grew but to call attention to characteristics related to growth in the black middle class that have been overlooked.

The political impetus for black middle-class growth is embodied in four vehicles that implemented federal legislation and policies that enhanced the status of blacks: the Equal Employment Opportunity Commission, the Office of Federal Contract Compliance Programs, federal contract set-aside programs, and federally funded social welfare expansion.

Equal Employment Opportunity Commission

Title VII of the 1964 Civil Rights Act provided the muscle for federal attempts to eradicate employment bias in the United States, establishing the Equal Employment Opportunity Commission (EEOC) as the law's administrative agency. The EEOC required private firms with one hundred or more employees to report numbers of minority workers to the commission. Federal contractors with fifty or more employees and federal contractors or subcontractors selling goods or services worth at least $50,000 also are covered by the law. At the start, the EEOC was authorized to use "informal methods" to resolve complaints of job discrimination. But by 1972 the enforcement powers granted to the EEOC by Congress gave it the right to initiate civil suits in district courts. By 1973, the EEOC gained further leverage in the private sector by winning a consent decree from American Telephone and Telegraph (AT&T) agreeing to pay $38 million to workers discriminated against by the company (Hill 1977). At the same time, the EEOC created a system that tracked discrimination and "patterns and practices" charges against limited numbers of large employers (Purcell 1977). This demonstration of the EEOC's serious intent was a major impetus for corporate employers to seek black labor. Richard Freeman (1976:136) reported that "federally required programs involving job quotas that favor minorities have made minority hiring an explicit goal of major corporations. At IBM for example, every manager is told that his annual performance evaluation includes a report on his success in meeting Affirmative Action goals." In Heidrick and Struggles's (1979b) survey of Fortune 500 companies 52 percent who responded reported in 1979 that achievement of affirmative-action goals was a factor in reviewing management compensation. General Electric's policy sanctions and Sears's Mandatory Achievement of Goals program represent similar force-fed structural changes to increase black employment.

Comparing firms reporting to the EEOC with the total data reported by the National Commission for Manpower Policy for the years 1966 through 1974, Andrew Brimmer (1976) concluded that companies reporting under EEOC requirements opened jobs to blacks much faster than did nonreporting firms. Thus, in the eyes of white employers, the status of black workers was apparently enhanced. Other studies found that Title VII had a strong effect on the employment status of blacks in the private sector (Freeman 1973; Haworth, Gwartney, and Haworth 1975). Heckman (1976) found the effect of fair employment practices on employment status strongly significant. Purcell (1977) noted that at AT&T, the figures for blacks in second-level management and above increased 126 percent between 1972 and 1975 as a result of the company's different approach to employment.

Federal Contract Compliance

Additional federal government influence on white private sector employment policy is exercised through federal contracts, which also enhanced economic opportunities for blacks. Business enterprises with federal contracts or subcontracts of $50,000 or more were compelled to comply with federal hiring guidelines or face the withdrawal of federal money. Although loss of contract through noncompliance was a sanction of last resort and not well documented, 45 percent of all Fortune 500 companies reported that they had been threatened with ineligibility on compliance issues (Heidrick and Struggles 1979). I believe, therefore, that the threat alone was enough to change private-sector employment practices.

Comparative research during the 1970s on the impact of contract compliance in the white private sector found that government contractors hired significantly more black males than did nongovernment contractors. Ashenfelter and Heckman (1976) found that in the short run government contractors raised the employment of blacks relative to white males 3.3 percent more than did nongovernmental contractors. In the long run this effect was estimated to be 12.9 percent. Research also noted that more government contracts were awarded to less discriminatory firms (Heckman and Wolpin 1976) and that segregated white contractors were more likely to integrate than segregated white noncontractors (Ashenfelter and Heckman 1976).

More recent studies also have found that federal contract compliance programs significantly improved employment opportunities for blacks. Heckman and Payner (1989) found similar benefits in their study of the South Carolina textile industry when they isolated the specific effects of antidiscrimination laws from other programs and economic events that occurred at the same time. Leonard (1982) used establishment-level EEO-1 reports (filed by EEOC-covered employers) on more than sixteen million employees for 1974 and 1980 and establishment-level affirmative action compliance review reports for the period 1973 to 1981 to compare a matched sample of contractors with noncontractors. He found blacks' share of employment with government contractors grew significantly more than at noncontractor establishments, and that federal contract compliance programs substantially improved the employment opportunities for black men in particular. He argues that affirmative action supported the rise of the black middle class by increasing the demand for black labor in higher-paying, white-collar jobs relative to blue-collar, operative, and laborer occupations. Herring and Collins (1995) analyzed the 1990 General Social Survey and a 1992 survey of Chicago adults and also found affirmative action associated with higher occupational prestige for African Americans and with substantial incremental effects on the incomes of racial minorities.

Federal Procurement

The growth of the black middle class since the 1960s is also related to the government's own hiring efforts. For example, federal depart-

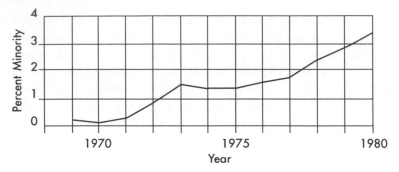

Figure 3. Federal Minority Procurement: 1969–1980

ments such as the Department of Commerce established specialized minority procurement procedures known as the contract set-aside program (U.S. Department of Commerce 1979). Before guidelines covered such transactions, government contracts for vast amounts of consumer goods and services were awarded almost exclusively to white-owned businesses. The set-aside program established the percent of government contracts that should go to minority-owned businesses, in an effort to assist businesses historically hindered by their inability to secure capital from white banks and to compete outside black communities. These programs helped to expand both the size and type of black firms by giving black entrepreneurs a chance to compete for sizable contracts in a protected setting.

In fiscal year 1969, minority business participants in federal procurement accounted for only .03 percent of total dollar awards, a figure that dramatically increased from 1969 to 1973, after President Nixon established the Office of Minority Business Enterprise. The gains are presented in Figure 3, which also shows how fluctuations in minority business procurement coincide with changes in White House administrations. The percentage of minority business participation in direct and indirect contracting decreased in 1974 and remained constant at approximately 1.4 percent of total procurement until 1976, a period when no policies addressed federalwide goals for minority procurement. Any goals were local ones, if established at all.

In 1977, President Carter created the Interagency Council for Minority Business Enterprise as the principal instrument to coordinate federal purchases from minority firms; its palpable effect was to increase procurement from 1977 through 1980. Data from the U.S. Department of Commerce (1981b) indicate that as a result of contract set-asides, the amount of goods and services sold by minority firms to federal agencies grew from $3 million in 1969 to $3 billion in 1980.[3]

The probable effects of federal initiatives (and contract set-aside programs started on other levels of government) on the black business sector also show up in comparisons of gross receipts of majority- and minority-owned firms between 1969 and 1977. For example, between 1969 and 1972 minority business revenue increased by 57 percent, majority firms by 24.5 percent. During the same period, the proportion of black firms increased in almost every industry, as did the black percent of all firms' gross receipts (U.S. Department of Commerce 1981a). Here again are changes that suggest a relationship between the race-based economic policy during this period and the enhanced overall competitiveness of minority businesses.

Social Service Expansion

In addition to contract set-aside programs, new arenas for black employment also emerged as public welfare services and federally funded, black-run community organizations grew. According to William Wilson (1978) more than two thousand community action programs were formed during the War on Poverty. Some of these sprang from grass-roots concerns, others were government created.

Between the early 1960s and the middle 1970s, the public sector grew and social service bureaucracies, especially, proliferated. Estimates have been made that at least two-thirds of the recent growth in public employment can be attributed to social welfare programs. Brown and Erie (1981) connected the expanding educational bureaucracy to the programs of the Great Society era (e.g., the Elementary and Secondary Education Act, the inauguration of Head Start, and other preschool programs authorized by the Economic Opportunity Act). In addition, federal government increased funding to social programs in medical, public housing, and manpower-training areas, which also contributed to the growth of the public sector.[4]

This growth in federal bureaucracy occurred at least in part because blacks demanded that the poor had the right to receive welfare subsidies and that the government must provide them. The political origin of the War on Poverty has been confirmed by several authors (Donovan 1967; Levitan 1969; Piven and Cloward 1971; Yarmolinsky 1967). And, although federal welfare programs were not created exclusively for blacks, the public views them as attempts to meet black needs for more economic and social resources. One might, for example, view the War on Poverty as a response to the existence of various urban, not black, problems. But Piven and Cloward (1971:258–259) show that many urban problems occurred equally in rural areas, yet the Office of Economic Opportunity concentrated funds in large urban centers, where blacks are concentrated. Federal remedial programs affecting elementary and secondary education, such as Operation Head Start, were directed primarily at black children. In addition, the criteria for participating in dependency-related services such as the food stamp program and in welfare programs such as Aid to Families with Dependent Children were oriented toward blacks. In general, the expanding network of urban social services favored blacks because of their lower incomes. For example, inner-city blacks disproportionately tended to benefit from increased health, hospital, welfare, and public housing services.

Government was a significant employer of blacks even before the 1960s. But public settings seemed to strengthen that role when government at every level expanded the social service bureaucracy in that decade. In 1960, 13.3 percent of employed blacks worked for government; in 1970, 21.4 percent; and in 1979, 24 percent. Between 1960 and 1979, the proportion of employed blacks in government positions increased at twice the rate of whites. The relative chances of blacks and whites for being employed in government rose in these two decades from about equal probability to more than one-third more likely that blacks would be so employed. Robert Althauser's (1975) study of black and white graduates in the 1970s found that, indeed, black graduates tended to gravitate toward public sector jobs in larger proportions than white graduates.

As a result of these race-oriented programs, the black middle class made economic and social gains. As noted previously, the proportion of employed black men working in professional, technical, and managerial positions doubled between 1960 and 1979. Between 1960 and 1970 the probability of black as compared to white managers to be in government rose 67 percent, although the overall odds of employed blacks to be in government decreased slightly (U.S. Bureau of the Census 1963; 1973). Between 1960 and 1970, for example, the proportion of black managers and officials employed by government increased about 30 percent; in contrast, white proportions decreased by 15 percent. In 1960, 13 percent of white managers and 21 percent of black managers and administrators worked in government. By 1970, 27 percent of black managers but just 11 percent of white managers worked in government. Whether this increase is due to upgrading employed blacks or to an influx of black managers cannot be determined. Nevertheless, it seems evident that government directly contributed to blacks' enhanced economic opportunities, particularly in the higher-paying white-collar occupations. Between 1960 and 1982 the proportion of black men who were public employees rose to about twice the proportion of white men in managerial and administrative occupations (U.S. Bureau of the Census 1963, 1973; U.S. Bureau of Labor Statistics 1982).

The relationship between growth of the federal bureaucracy and the elevation of blacks' economic status is not a new one. During the era of the New Deal, for example, the proportion of blacks employed in the government more than doubled. A slightly higher proportion of blacks was represented in the government work force than the proportion of blacks in the population. According to Sitkoff (1978:76), "The New Deal . . . opened up professional opportunities on a grand scale for blacks in the federal government. Negroes worked in the New Deal as architects, economists, engineers, lawyers, librarians, office managers, and statisticians." It is not surprising, then, that increased government employment accounts for many of the significant changes in black employment patterns during the 1960s. Black accountants, engineers, lawyers, personnel workers, social scientists, and managers are all twice as likely as whites to be in government. Further, in 1980 close to half (47 percent) of employed black professionals and technicians worked in the government sector as compared to only 34 percent of whites employed in the same categories (U.S. Bureau of Labor Statistics 1982).

The demand for skilled blacks within the public sector is also reflected in statistics showing that in 1969, minorities held 7.8 percent of federal jobs at grades GS9 through GS11, while in 1975 this figure had almost doubled to 12 percent (Hampton 1977). The pay range for these positions was $20,000 to $32,000 in 1975 (Hampton 1977). Freeman's (1976a) estimate of black and white incomes for 1966 and 1969 shows that black, but not white, public employees earned more than their privately employed peers. Eccles (1975) reported that the ratios of black to white income in government were above the economywide average for college graduates.

Although the earning ratio between blacks in the public and private sectors decreased, in 1979 the median salaries of blacks in government continued to be higher than the median for blacks in private nonagricultural jobs by 25 percent (U.S. Bureau of the Census 1980a). According to Norman Seary, past executive director of the Voluntary Organization of Blacks in Government, 55 percent of all blacks in the federal work force in 1980 fit categories of professional, managerial, and technical workers earning $30,000 to $37,000 a year (Poole 1981).

The movement of middle-class blacks into traditionally closed market situations can be viewed optimistically as evidence that economic opportunities (i.e., jobs and income) associated with class position are mediated more by education and skills, and less restricted by barriers that are related to race. However, with few exceptions (Brown and Erie 1981; Collins 1983), existing studies fail to credit the activities of government in their analysis of factors that increased job opportunities for blacks. At this point, however, the relationship between federal government initiatives and blacks' economic mobility is clear.

The growth of the black middle class during the 1960s and 1970s, occurred in a peculiar way. Black advancement was greatest in the government and in the segments of private industry that responded to government equal employment initiatives. A picture emerges of black middle-class growth in which federal government policy has an important effect on the labor market for blacks.

Farley (1977) noted that gains made among blacks in the 1960s did not diminish in the economically stagnant 1970s. The significance of the "policy factor" is that it explains this phenomenon without removing the importance of race. Market demands in this period were not just for labor, but for black labor. Although the economy fluctuated, federal social policy oriented toward the improvement of blacks' social status fluctuated less.

Growth of this politically mediated labor market, however, contrasts with that in a free-market situation, which (hypothetically) employs labor in response to consumer rather than government preferences. The labor market of the 1960s and 1970s was essentially a product of federal dollars, which restructured market demands for black labor. The distinction is important if one assumes that race discrimination remains active, in which case the withdrawal of federal supports would erode this class position. In the 1990s, if blacks and whites were to lose jobs in the federal government in equal numbers, for instance, the impact on blacks would be substantially more dramatic. Despite optimism over the emergence of economic opportunities for blacks in the middle class since the 1960s, other authors have expressed this reservation. Freeman (1976a) predicted more than two decades ago that if government pressures for affirmative action weakened, so might the demand for black college personnel. The link between the growth of the black middle class and public policy highlights both the dependency and the fragility of the class position.

Chapter 3

Racialized Services in the Workplace

✦ The 1980s ushered in the "Reagan revolution," a sharp reversal in the liberal democratic thinking that had dominated federal domestic social policy for fifty years. To understand just how vulnerable the black middle class is when federal policies change, it is necessary to define "racialized" services as they occur in policy- and in market-motivated situations. I define as racialized any services directed at, disproportionately used by, or concerned with blacks. Conversely, "mainstream" services are directed at, used by, or concerned with any consumer. For example, black-owned advertising firms are segregated in the market sector via links to black consumers. Administrators and professionals in public sector settings such as Chicago's Department of Human Services are in segregated situations because they are linked to dependent blacks.

I believe that, by the 1980s, most jobs that allowed the black middle-class to move ahead were disproportionately racialized, part of a system of tasks that would nullify blacks' potential for disruption. The idea of public and corporate substructures managed in response to local political pressures is not new (Piven and Cloward 1971, 1977). But I apply the idea here to argue that a black middle class of public and private sector functionaries was useful to white power structures during the 1960s and 1970s while at the same time occupying a precarious market position. The following data lend support to this idea.

When black political action disrupted the social and economic order during the 1960s, the response of white power structures was to develop social welfare, community development, and employment policies and programs to reinstate order. Two trends are notable in the occupational shifts made by black male college graduates between 1960 and 1970 (U.S. Bureau of the Census 1963, 1973). First, they made progress in almost every occupation outside the professions traditionally filled by blacks, such as social welfare and teaching. In 1950, only 61 percent of nonwhite male graduates were professionals or managers compared with 74 percent of all college men. By 1970, the ratio was 75 percent compared with 80 percent. In contrast, college-trained black women have traditionally had very similar job distributions to those of their white peers. In a second trend, college-educated black men moved into occupations where they could calm disruptive black elements of the population. Among selected professional occupations where employed black men with four or more years of college were underrepresented compared to whites in 1960, only two show gains that *exceed* the white proportion in 1970: personnel and labor relations, and public relations (U.S. Bureau of the Census 1963, 1973). The largest increases for black men in the 1960s occurred in personnel and labor relations jobs (400 percent) and public relations (300 percent); next in rank were social scientists (70 percent) and social welfare workers (67 percent). Without much more detail about what these work roles involved, the pattern appears consistent with my hypothesis. These gains are in occupations that have people-related, as opposed to technical, functions. If the white power structure during the 1960s was concerned about managing the upheaval among blacks, these are the kinds of jobs for which blacks would be in demand to manage or administer institutions, or organization units, where the white power structure mediates the needs of black consumers or the black work force. Significant portions of black middle-class income would thus rely on jobs dependent on heavy concentrations of blacks. Black service or product providers whose activities depend heavily on transactions with other blacks as clients have racialized jobs. Black supervisors overseeing a predominantly black work force also are racialized.

Racialized Roles in the Public Sector

Although few if any products, services, or policies in the public sector are consumed solely by blacks, some are consumed by much higher proportions of the black population than the white. Criteria for participation in dependency-related services such as food stamps and Aid to Families with Dependent Children were explicitly oriented toward blacks. Other services aimed at lower-income households differentially favor blacks. Low-income blacks tend to be overrepresented among those who use public facilities and services such as public housing, health and hospital care, corrections, and city transportation systems.

The legislative response to blacks' protest during the 1960s was to distribute subsidies to industries and portions of industries that dependent blacks use.[1] Besides pacifying the black underclass, these subsidies expanded the work settings and increased the level of incomes available to blacks in the middle class. Blacks working in racialized services were the indirect beneficiaries of the expansion of social services. At the same time, blacks employed in these services were intermediaries between white institutions and other blacks through racialized services, for social policy oriented toward blacks was funneled through them.

If my hypothesis about opportunities for black employment is correct, one would expect concentration in the services indicated above. Underrepresentation should occur in services oriented toward the more mainstream consumer. Public employment data from the U.S. Equal Employment Opportunity Commission (1980a) generally conformed to this expectation. In 1978 blacks made up only 20 percent of all city employees, nationwide. Yet blacks were 35 percent of city hospital workers, 34 percent of all city health workers, and, remarkably, 50 percent of all public welfare employees. Similar patterns existed on the state level. Although blacks made up only 14 percent of all public employees at the state level nationwide, in 1978 18 percent of all public welfare workers, 23 percent of all hospital workers, and 49 percent of all housing employees were black. Conversely, blacks made up only 11 percent of all financial administration workers, 7 percent of street and highway workers, and 5 percent of natural resource employees. On both state and local levels, sanitation and sewage workers represent the single category in which blacks were heavily concentrated in a mainstream rather than a racialized service. (This, however, accords with my idea of segregation by occupation. Sanitation services are useful for absorbing high proportions of unskilled black labor.) Comparing the proportion of all black and white workers in city and state government in 1978 showed that when job functions correspond to the expected disproportionately high use of a service or facility by blacks, black employees tend to be overrepresented. In cities, the black proportion employed in hospitals and public housing was more than twice that of whites, and about three times more in corrections. These figures create a striking picture in which blacks' economic opportunities were overconcentrated in race-oriented job functions.

A similar picture emerged on the state level. When job functions coincided with heavy black use of services, blacks were far more likely than whites to hold such jobs. Conversely, for jobs more likely to serve a general consumer, blacks had much less likelihood than whites to be employed. The single exception, again, was sanitation and sewage workers, where functions serve a general public. The extent to which this service was ghettoized in 1978 was remarkable. Blacks were eleven times more likely than whites to be employed in this function.

Within the context of this study, a better test of my hypothesis is to remove lower-status workers (clerical, blue-collar, and service) from the picture and focus on full-time professional, administrative, and appointed workers. (In this discussion I use the term *professional* to cover these categories.) The general picture remained the same (see Table 1).

Blacks were overrepresented in professional positions where race and economic status differentially defined consumer populations. On the city level, for example, black professionals were three times as likely as whites to be employed in public welfare and corrections, twice as likely to be employed in hospitals and health, and more

Table 1
Black and White Professionals, Administrators, and Officials: 1978 (percentage)

	City		State	
Agency	Black	White	Black	White
Public Welfare	15	3	22	15
Corrections	3	1	13	7
Hospitals	22	11	15	13
Health	7	4	10	11
Housing	5	3	1	.20
Community Development	4	4	1	.70
Sanitation and Sewage	3	3	*	*
Financial Administration	14	18	13	17
Police	4	12	4	2
Streets and Highways	2	5	3	10
Natural Resources	8	6	2	8
Utility and Transportation	3	8	.40	1
Fire	3	17	*	*
Employment Security	*	*	11	9
Other	6	4	4	6
Total†	99	99	99	100

Source: U.S. Equal Employment Opportunity Commission (1980a)
*Not reported, or less than 0.5 percent.
†Totals do not add up to 100 percent due to rounding and nonreported figures.

likely to be employed in housing. At the state level, black professionals were disproportionately concentrated in public welfare, corrections, and housing, although this service employed only a small number of either race. Black professionals were also somewhat overrepresented in hospitals and employment security. It is not surprising that they were only one and one-half times as likely as whites to be in state-administered public welfare services, given that state welfare offices, which tend to be scattered in small communities, are less anchored than their urban counterparts to large concentrations of black people. In a similar vein, state employment offices must meet the needs of a widely dispersed population. In both cases there is theoretically less implicit reason for blacks to be employed.

That black middle-class employment in the public sector was anchored to black populations is significant because it thus depended on vulnerable subsidies. Mainstream functions, such as police and fire, tend to depend on revenue generated through locally controlled city or state resources such as taxes or revolving funds. Racialized public services were heavily or entirely dependent upon revenue controlled at the federal level. This issue on its own would not be critical were it not that racialized programs addressed the needs of populations that were dependent and powerless (unless disruptive). Negotiations for funds take place in a political arena whose response to this population is unpredictable. Dependency-related services, like their recipients, were vulnerable to racial politics. Income from these services is essentially the "soft money" in government payrolls.

In the early years of the Reagan presidency the fifty-year trend of more and more federal dominance in social program areas was reversed. The Chicago Department of Human Services exemplifies the effects of subsequent shifts in federal funding on job stability. The department performed "public welfare" services for the city during the early 1980s, and its funding came from both city (corporate) and federal (program) revenue. Federal money supported the agency's social service arm, heavily used by dependent blacks. Corporate funds supported the agency's administrative functions. Almost all of the income for professional staff was generated by federal money, whereas only the top levels of management were supported by corporate funds. In a *Chicago Tribune* article, "Minority City Workers First to Go in Reagan's Aid Cuts," that appeared on 14 December 1981 local officials explained that "the policy of placing minority workers on federally funded payrolls ensures that most of the city employees to be laid off because of budget cuts will be black and Hispanic." Of the 400 employees laid off at the Chicago Department of Human Services during that time period, approximately 75.9 percent were black. Similarly, of the 186 workers laid off from the Department of Health, almost 40 percent were black. In contrast, the Streets and Sanitation Department, where funding is generated more locally, showed few effects from the federal cutbacks. The

Chicago Sun Times reported on 29 March 1981, under the headline "Minority, Female Job Gains Periled," that this department was only 20 percent black in 1981.

General employment opportunities for professionals can be measured by comparing their distribution in various public functions. For example, city housing services employed a larger proportion of all city professionals (3 percent) than did state housing (.2 percent). Conversely, city health services employed a smaller proportion of all professionals (4 percent) than did health services at the state level (11 percent). Comparing city with state functions that tend to perform racialized services, such as public welfare, the smaller the percentage of total employed, the greater the odds that blacks will be employed. For example, in 1982, states employed 15 percent of all full-time professionals in welfare functions; cities employed only 5 percent. Yet the proportion of blacks to whites was almost four times greater at the local level. The same pattern held true for hospital, health, and corrections.

An apparent explanation for this employment pattern is that blacks tend to find jobs where the black population is concentrated and where they exercise political power. In many large cities, then as now, blacks and other minorities make up over one-half of the total population. At the same time however, cities in general are more revenue dependent than are states. Therefore, in terms of both occupation and government level, blacks are concentrated in fiscally vulnerable situations.

The link between black employment in the public sector and black populations increases this vulnerability. Public jobs are responsive to both community demands and political pressures. For example, the *Chicago Sun Times* reported on 12 December 1994 in an article headed "Hispanics Condemn Lack of School Jobs" that between 1989 and 1994 African Americans in Chicago's public sector lost ground in policy-making city jobs, while whites, Hispanics, and Asians made sizable gains: The proportion of African Americans decreased by 13 percent, as whites, Hispanics, and Asians gained by 28 percent, 85 percent, and 82 percent respectively, although the base point for Asian Americans was low. One explanation for this shift is that other urban groups have begun using the political strategies that during the 1960s and 1970s produced results for African Americans. That is, they apply political pressure to increase access to, or to protect, institutional privilege. In 1994, for example, Hispanic activist groups in Chicago demanded that more Hispanics be hired as administrators and teachers in the city's public schools, necessarily replacing African Americans then disproportionately represented in this job pool. Similarly, in Los Angeles, Hispanic activist groups targeted jobs in the U.S. Post Office, a job resource that in the not-too-distant past contributed to the economic stability of blacks and to blacks' ability to be middle class.

Similar activity can be found among other ethnic groups (Ramos 1994). In a politically mediated opportunity structure, public jobs are resources that can be oriented toward one group or another to satisfy demands. In the 1980s and the 1990s, protests organized by more politically active coalitions of labor work to the detriment of now mollified African Americans.

Segregated employment patterns to appease black demands were also suggested in employment data on federal-level jobs in 1980. The departments of Housing and Urban Development, Health and Human Services, and Community Services Administration showed heavy concentrations of black employees (U.S. Equal Employment Opportunity Commission 1980a). For example, of the Community Services Administration's nine hundred employees, 44 percent were black (U.S. Equal Employment Opportunity Commission 1980b). This is precisely the type of agency that sprang up to absorb black demands for increased social and economic resources in the sixties; it was abolished by 1982. These data do not tell us if blacks were already concentrated in these types of public services and moved up into professional and administrative positions, or if they were pulled into these positions as part of employers' response to 1960s political activism. Although the data and calculations suffer from weaknesses, the analysis tends to support the argument that, by the 1980s, much of the gain made in the middle class in professional and managerial jobs occurred in public settings where policy absorbed black demands.

Some obvious questions unanswered by these data eventually led me to collect the qualitative data on which most of this book is based. For instance, were blacks concentrated in black-oriented services and functions because they preferred these to mainstream opportunities or because these represented the job avenues with least resistance to blacks' entry? In addition, these data, in contrast to the qualitative data presented in Chapter 5, do not allow us a close enough look at the workplace to measure racialized pockets, even within mainstream functions.

Racialized Roles in the Black-Owned Business Sector

Government policy inspired growth in the black business sector during the 1960s and 1970s, as well as in the public sector. Data available also suggest that black entrepreneurs held racialized rather than mainstream market niches by the late 1970s. The great preponderance of black-owned business (98 percent) remained concentrated in retail and selected services where, historically, black businesses have been forced to market their wares almost exclusively to black consumers; a sizable proportion of all minority business is based either on federal procurement or on sales to the minority community (U.S. Department of Commerce 1979). A 2 April 1982 *Chicago Tribune* article, "Report Urges Business Aid for Minorities," typical of media coverage at the time, reported that minority business owners pushed for federal aid to help black firms penetrate general (i.e., white) consumer markets, an indication that black businesses were relegated to the limited growth markets in inner-city neighborhoods and tied to public aid income, as they remain today. Thus racialized, they are useful for serving low-income blacks in potentially volatile environments. In addition, they are indirectly linked to policy fluctuation which adversely affects disadvantaged blacks.

Even when federal policy on black business development stimulated expansion among nontraditional service businesses during the 1970s, the hypothesis should still hold that black entrepreneurs concentrate in areas where they hold racialized and functional positions related to black populations. Black businesses represented in the *Chicago United Compendium of Professional Services* (1980) not only typify nontraditional firms in 1980 but were publicly acknowledged successes. To be included in the 1980 compendium was one measure of professional and business competence. One could reasonably expect these successful and nontraditional firms to be the most likely to join those serving the mainstream consumer market. Businesses listed there further illustrate the intersection of black business functions and market demands.

The compendium, published in 1980, lists blacks in three advertising firms, five architecture and engineering firms, six management consultation firms, three certified public accounting firms, four law firms, and seven personal services firms. All except two firms listed were established between 1965 and 1979. Most, therefore, are firms in which blacks were able to capitalize on race-related market incentives. The two exceptions were an advertising firm established in 1950 and an accounting firm established in 1939. The following excerpts describe these firms and illustrate the type of market they cornered:

> [Advertising firm] offers the following services: marketing planning, marketing research, media planning and buying, creative services, print and broadcast.

> [Advertising firm] is a full-service Chicago based advertising agency primarily concerned with the black consumer market. Selected Clients: Coca-Cola (U.S.A.) and McDonalds.

> [Architect and engineer], general experience covers: urban renewal clearance, housing programs, conversion projects, municipal planning. Selected Clients: City of Gary Indiana and Public Building Commission of Chicago.

> [Management consultant] . . . provides management consultant and public relations services . . . on employment practices and affirmative action programs for minorities and women. Selected Clients: People's Gas and Joint Legislative Administrative Committee on Public Aid.

[Certified public account firm] has been under contract with the City of Chicago to perform pre-grant award audits — as well as financial audits of agencies and grantors under federally funded programs. Selected Clients: City of Chicago, Office of the City Controller and Commonwealth Edison.

[Legal services] . . . land transactions, secured commercial transactions, the defense of property claims collections, contract compliance, casualty claims and labor-management problems. Selected Clients: United States Department of Housing and Urban Development and Mammoth Life and Accident Insurance Company.

[Personnel service] . . . specialization is minority recruitment in all areas of employment. Selected Clients: Honeywell and International Harvester.

The first thing that is apparent from the descriptions is that these firms were performing services comparable to those offered by their majority competitors. That is, the advertising firms do market research, and the engineers plan building sites. Not only do these firms show clientele from the black private sector (Mammoth Life), but they show relationships with Coca-Cola, Honeywell, and People's Gas as well. And second, most were depending on racialized services to draw their mainstream consumers. For example, the advertising firm capitalizes on its black consumer market, while other types of firms address the corporate response to equal employment opportunity in hiring and promotion. These were the services that were most expected to attract business from the majority corporate world.

Since the compendium offered only short descriptions of business functions, I conducted telephone interviews in 1982 with one professional representative from each black firm listed. I asked general questions about whether the firm did business with any sector not mentioned among "selected clients," and what kinds of services were performed for clients. For example, if all clients listed in the compendium were from the white corporate sector, I asked whether business was done with public and black private clients as well. I

Table 2

Nontraditional Black Firms in Racialized and General Services

	Service	
Client	Racialized*	General†
Public	A E M M M M C C L L L	E E E C P
White Private	A A A M M M M L L P P P P	E E C C C L P P
Black Private	M C C C L L L L L P P P A	
Total	36	13

Note: The following symbols are used to indicate type of firm: A = Advertising (*N* = 3); C = Certified Public Accounting (*N* = 3); E = Engineering and Architecture (*N* = 5); L = Law (*N* = 4); M = Management Consulting (*N* = 5); P = Personnel Services (*N* = 6).

*The racialized category includes the services directed at black consumer/manpower needs.

†The general category includes services directed at a general population/market.

also asked for examples of the kinds of work a firm performed in each sector. Based on the services that were described, I then decided whether or not the service was generally black related. For example, I placed accounting firms involved in establishing general accounting systems in the Zenith Corporation in the mainstream category of services, and accounting firms establishing systems for certain types of federal contracts in the racialized category of services. One firm was establishing an accounting system for a California regional office to be used specifically for Comprehensive Employment and Training Act (CETA) funds. CETA program funds, of course, targeted blacks. Table 2 shows the sector distribution of these firms' clients and whether or not they were related to racialized (R) or mainstream (G) services. Type of service was categorized for each sector in which the firm was involved. If a sector involved services in both categories (R and G), the firm appears in both. All firms doing business with other black firms were automatically classified as racialized, along with their other sector involvement.

Even discounting firms' dependence on the black market, Table 2 illustrates that they show up in racialized business services more often than not. Of course, this is an overly simplified categorization.

I did not ask businesses how many contracts they received from where, to do what, and with what profit margins. Nevertheless the table is a beginning effort to show that the strongest foothold outside black markets occurred in "black specialties" offered to white institutions. Black law firms negotiated on behalf of their white corporate client when affirmative action or federal contract compliance was at issue, or when white firms were entering contract negotiations with black proprietors or land owners, or when insurance claims for the black insured needed settling. Black personnel service and management consulting firms were almost exclusively involved in black manpower development and executive search for white corporations. Black management consulting firms also helped in the political negotiations of corporations establishing services in the black community. Black advertising firms helped white corporations exclusively to penetrate black consumer markets. Roles were race specified even among firms that dealt with white corporate structures in mainstream functions. Engineering firms with business in the white sector entered into these relationships as subcontractors, based on the corporate need to hire minority firms to compete for federal contracts. Although these functions show up in the General category, it can be debated whether or not they belong there.

Even in the public sector, firms were drawn into performing racialized services. Personnel service firms provided workers for such ghettoized agencies as the Office of Manpower, and law firms were hired for contract compliance and labor-management issues in such racialized services as the Department of Housing and Urban Development. Certified public accountant firms performed pregrant audits and general audits for racialized institutions such as Cook County Hospital. Management consulting firms provided technical assistance primarily to ghettoized units such as the Department of Human Services or the Office of Minority Business Development. Engineers provided professional services to ghettoized manpower sites such as the Northshore Sanitary District. These firms were relatively successful products of moral and legislative commitments made in the past few decades to establish greater exchange between white corporations and black enterprise. Yet even here black businesses appeared to be useful only when they served in symbolic or intermediary positions between white structures and black clients. The degree to which these firms competed in the corporate world on the basis of company profit, as opposed to policy, predicts the softness of their market position. Past growth in government-let contracts, coupled with stipulations for black subcontractors, helped form a mutually beneficial relationship. However, when public policy changed and profit considerations encompassed broader issues as the 1980s progressed, this alliance probably changed.

Racialized Roles in the White Private Sector

Salaried blacks employed in the white private sector showed similar relationships to those in the public sector in the late 1970s and early 1980s. A 1979 survey of Fortune 500 companies reported that more than 29 percent of black executives versus 3 percent of white were in personnel specialties (Heidrick and Struggles 1979b). These are positions in the corporate structure typically responsible for affirmative-action plans and implementation. An example of how companies used such positions lies in the Coca-Cola and Heublein negotiations with People United to Save Humanity's (PUSH) trade association in 1982. In 1971, Jesse Jackson launched PUSH covenant negotiations to expand opportunities for black individuals and business. Some of these negotiations took place with black community affairs officers who were viewed by PUSH representatives as major stumbling blocks to PUSH objectives for these corporations. In general, not only were these positions functional in dealing with the problem of blacks, they were an effective way for corporate entities to address government hiring policies while minimizing black power. Personnel, labor relations, and public relations officials operate outside the strategic planning or production areas that typically lead to power within the corporation. They are the "soft money" within the business world.

Over 22 percent of black executives in Fortune 500 companies in 1979 were in manufacturing, a category that nationwide accounted for the second largest industrial concentration of black labor (Heidrick and Struggles 1979b; U.S. Bureau of Labor Statistics 1982). One might suppose that these executives were useful in managing large numbers of blacks, while helping the companies meet affirmative action requirements (Fernandez 1981). At the same time they were concentrated in the "soft" sector of the economy in an arena of jobs that experienced a steep decline. As public policy is reversed, the implicit need for blacks in these kinds of positions may also diminish.

Taken together, these data tend to support the idea that in the 1960s and 1970s the black middle class became economically dependent on governmental policy and programs instituted to deal with black unrest. In the late 1970s, black public sector employees were concentrated in the portions of government operations that legitimized and subsidized black underclass dependency, such as social welfare institutions. In the black private sector, black-owned businesses remained concentrated in economically underdeveloped areas or dependent on policy-supported joint ventures with white firms or in protected and racialized consumer markets. Salaried blacks in the private sector seem to have been concentrated in intermediary positions between white corporations and black consumer, manpower, or policy issues.

The racial disparity in the structure of professional opportunities available to blacks is clear. In the years surrounding social upheaval among blacks, members of the black middle class, no longer restricted by occupation or income, remained segregated. In this system of segregation they were concentrated in institutions dependent on government subsidy and in race-oriented services. Thus, by 1980 race was strongly implicated in blacks' economic position in the U.S. economy, despite the obvious ascent of blacks into middle-class positions.

Chapter 4

Tan Territories, Urban Upheaval, and the New Black Professionals

> Question: How did you find your job in personnel management for [a major white-owned insurance company]?
>
> Answer: It was all luck. I was at an NAACP convention. They saw me and offered me a job right there on the spot [in 1966]. Over the next three to four years they hired twenty-five or thirty people like that. If you were black and walked by they'd just about grab you off the streets.
>
> —From an interview with a senior investment analyst and director employed in a venture capital division of a firm in the insurance industry

✦ A radical alteration occurred in the hiring practices of white-owned companies around the middle 1960s. Until then, black employment patterns in major industries reflected the U.S. cultural norm of de facto segregation and discrimination against black workers (Burstein 1985; Farley 1984; Jaynes and Williams 1989; Wilson 1978). Blacks disproportionately filled a job ghetto comprised of low-paying, physically demanding, and subservient blue-collar and service work for white private industry (McKersie n.d.; Wilson 1978).

In Chicago, blacks tended not to be placed in the principal office of multiestablishment firms; rarely did they fill white-collar jobs, such as sales and clerical jobs, and they were almost totally absent in professional and managerial jobs in white-dominated settings (McKersie n.d.). In Chicago in 1965, blacks were completely excluded from policy-making positions (Chicago Urban League 1977).

From about the mid-1960s onward, however, major white-owned corporations began to hire blacks into white-collar jobs — in particular, into previously closed professional and managerial positions. The term *previously closed* is borrowed from Richard Freeman (1976a:146) to characterize a particular change in the structure of jobs available to the black middle class, one in which blacks increased their proportion in business-related professions because they increasingly were recruited into white-owned, white-oriented economic settings. This juncture of breakthroughs (blacks' entry into new types of jobs and into new job settings) meant new job markets for the black middle class. During the 1960s and 1970s in the managerial world a new elite of blacks emerged as executives in major white corporations. In 1968, for instance, International Business Systems in New York hired into the engineering department the company's first black professional. A white New York corporate official candidly noted in a *Harvard Business Review* article in 1970, "I think we have reason to be a bit defensive about our past record. Thirty-five years ago we used to look for Germans and Swiss, even for the lowest level jobs. Then during World War II, we began to hire the Irish. By the time fighting broke out in Korea, we were taking Italians and Jews. Now we're actively recruiting blacks and Puerto Ricans" (Cohn 1975:11). Between 1960 and 1983, the proportion of black male college graduates employed in managerial jobs increased from 7 percent to 18 percent (Freeman 1976b; U.S. Bureau of Labor Statistics 1983). The executives I interviewed were at the forefront of this trend in the private sector. One director of personnel reported that when a major food manufacturer hired him in 1968 he was the only black college graduate in the Cincinnati corporate offices. Moreover, he was the first black ever in the company's management training program. Another personnel manager for a major national manufacturer reported that, in 1970, he became the first black promoted to manager in the Chicago location of the company. One ranking man was the first black professional a Fortune 50 company employed and, in 1968, the first to work in the Chicago corporate office. A fourth man, a high-level executive who works for a well-known consumer goods company, was one of the first five blacks the company employed in sales. He was hired in 1966, among the first of a large number of blacks hired by the company over the next six months.

One-half of the executives (thirty-six of seventy-three) I interviewed were the first blacks to integrate the professional and managerial job structure of a major white corporation at some level. Each entered the white private sector as the first black professional or manager hired by a company, either in the company's regional, state, city, or district offices or at specific company sites, such as corporate headquarters, plants, divisions, or departments. Even those who were not, technically, "firsts" were either one of only two or three blacks in a company's professional-managerial job structure, or part of the first cohort of blacks hired in the company's initial effort to recruit blacks into its professional-managerial ranks.

Some researchers explain the improved market for blacks by linking black employment to cyclic factors, pointing out that blacks' position in the labor market improves during economic expansion and declines during times of recession (Jaynes and Williams 1989; Levitan et al. 1975). Yet gains made by black workers in the professional-managerial job strata during the 1960s, under conditions of economic expansion, also increased during periods of recession in the 1970s (Farley 1977; Freeman 1976b). This phenomenon suggests that factors other than the economy play a crucial role in black attainment and provide countercyclic supports that sustain blacks' gains.

A second explanation suggests that improvements in the quality and quantity of education have been key to blacks' access to broader job opportunities (Smith and Welch 1986). However, they cannot solely account for the sudden inclusion of black Americans into higher-paying white-collar occupations in the 1960s. The quality of black education had increased from the 1940s onward (Jaynes and Williams 1989), and states and the federal government increased antidiscriminatory employment measures during the same postwar period. Moreover, before the 1960s, even similar educational achievement did not produce equality in black, relative to white, occupational attainment (McKersie n.d.); higher levels of black education actually accentuated some race-based economic differences (Siegel 1965; Thurow 1969).

These macroeconomic and human-capital explanations account for the presence of a pool of qualified black workers available to take advantage of the new opportunities, but they do not explain why those opportunities occurred when they did. Political interventions completed the equation and opened the job market. Human-capital theory views market dynamics as neutral, while I view the expansion of the black middle class during the 1960s and 1970s as a market response to corporate and state interventions intended to abate insurgency from below — a politically mediated phenomenon.

Job Markets for College-Educated Blacks

Contrary to popular public perception, until the 1960s, the most profound barriers to economic equality for blacks in the labor market were erected against college-educated and skilled blacks competing at the top of the economic hierarchy (Freeman 1976a). For instance, until the 1960s the absolute gap separating the earnings of black and white men actually increased as their amount of schooling increased (Farley 1984). One study indicates that racial differences in earnings in 1960 were almost five times as great for black men with college degrees as for black men who dropped out of elementary schools (Siegal 1965). Another classic study found that the earnings gap between college-educated black men and their white counterparts was about two and one-half times greater than the gap between black and white men with only eight years of education (Thurow 1969). A third highly influential study showed that the more years of schooling blacks had, the larger the gap between their purchasing power and that of comparably trained whites (Freeman 1976a). As late as 1959, the average earnings for nonwhite men with college educations was 20 percent lower than those of white male high school graduates (Freeman 1976a).

Not only pay discrimination but job restrictions severely limited the life chances and economic opportunities of college-educated blacks. For instance, before 1960 it was easier for unskilled and less-educated black workers to find jobs on the bottom rungs of the occupational ladder than for black college graduates to work in a white-dominated setting in more prestigious professional jobs. An illustration of this relative disparity appears in ethnographic accounts of discrimination in federal government employment at the end of World War II. Although statistical descriptions indicate that blacks in federal government jobs were not affected when white veterans returned home, the small number who held professional jobs in white-dominated government agencies were most likely to have their jobs threatened (Newman et al. 1978). In other words, blacks lost the small gains they had made during the war toward equality in federal employment and upward mobility. In contrast, blacks in low-status service jobs and black professionals in segregated settings fared better. For example, blacks did not lose out to returning white veterans who were low-status job holders, such as custodians, maintenance people, or laborers; they maintained gains made during the war in professional jobs in environments largely run and staffed by blacks, such as Freedman's Hospital (Newman et al. 1978; U.S. Senate 1954:204). In the 1950s, when more than one-third of employed nonwhite men were unskilled laborers or farm hands, the etiquette of workplace race relations held that college-educated blacks could not supervise whites or work immediately alongside them, nor could they work in any setting that was considered "refined" (Newman et al. 1978:33).

Overt racial discrimination and economic disincentives pervaded the job market in 1960. Consequently, in Chicago, African American men with enough education and experience to hold jobs equal to those of white men actually stood 15 percent lower on an economic index of occupational position (McKersie n.d.). Nationwide, college-educated black men were grossly underrepresented in the broad range of high-paying and high-status professions and virtually excluded from the business-related professions and the field of management. Only about 7 percent of nonwhite male college graduates in 1960 were managers compared to 18 percent of college-educated white men (Freeman 1976b:11). Blacks constituted less than 1 percent of accountants and engineers and just 1 percent of lawyers working in the United States. The absence of opportunities for college-educated blacks in the managerial and business-related professions is underscored by the failure of any major white corporation to make recruitment visits to historically black institutions in 1960 (Freeman 1976:35).[1] In this way, black college graduates were excluded from the pipeline that feeds the entry-level managerial and professional positions in large corporations. Effectively locked out of good jobs in white-owned industry, college-educated blacks were confined to a limited number of occupations that served the black community, such as physicians, teachers, and self-employed business owners (Drake and Cayton 1962; Frazier 1957).

During the mid-1960s, after a history of virtually total exclusion from better-paying jobs in white businesses, highly educated blacks were actively recruited by white corporations and experienced a striking transformation in the employment market demand. The longstanding pattern of decline in the income of educated blacks compared to whites was reversed. The ratio of black-to-white income rose most rapidly for managers. Between 1966 and 1970, the fraction of black men working as managers or professionals increased substantially, by 1970 almost doubling the 1960 numbers. The number of white corporations conducting employee searches at predominantly black colleges jumped dramatically after 1965 (Freeman 1976:35). In 1965, about thirty visits by white corporations to black college campuses took place. By 1970, the average black college campus received ten times that many visits. The same black colleges that corporations had shunned before the 1960s became an important source of black manpower recruitment in 1970.

Pre-1960s Job Markets

Although before the 1960s, skill and educational qualifications of black applicants had been important issues for white employers, placing high on these characteristics was not enough to eliminate employment discrimination. The individuals I interviewed were prepared by virtue of their education to start in professional and managerial jobs in private industry. Most of them (89 percent) had at least a bachelors degree when they entered the labor market. Over one-third (38 percent) had earned advanced degrees.

These proportions closely parallel the level of education of white male senior-level executives; 94 percent of top executives in Fortune 500 companies surveyed in 1986 had bachelors degrees; 42 percent had graduate degrees (Korn/Ferry 1986). Moreover, the level of education of my interviewees is well above the median level (about one year of college) for salaried male managers in 1960 (U.S. Bureau of the Census 1963). Slightly more than one-half of the black graduates I interviewed received their degrees from a predominantly white college or university. Yet a college education (as most other qualifications) failed to open corporate doors to prestigious and higher-paying jobs for those entering the labor market before the mid-1960s, compared to the jobs they held afterwards. Twenty-four of the twenty-nine (86 percent) who entered the labor market before 1965 had at least a four-year college degree, yet fewer than half got their first jobs in a white-owned establishment. Those who did work in the white private sector were concentrated in low-paying or segregated white-collar jobs, such as clerical and black-oriented sales occupations.

Private Sector Employment

The skewed midwestern labor market for blacks in the 1960s matched the national pattern, reflecting racial discrimination and the exclusion of blacks. In Chicago, as in the rest of the nation, blacks were placed in inconspicuous positions vis-à-vis the white public and were underrepresented in sales and clerical jobs. Their occupational position was much lower than that of similarly educated whites, and they were underrepresented in high-paying and high-status jobs (McKersie n.d.).

One case illustrating the underemployment faced by educated blacks is that of a marketing manager with a bachelor's degree in chemistry who expected to work with a major chemical company when he entered the midwest labor market in 1957. Instead, he says, "It was tremendously difficult to find that kind of job. . . . I had huge difficulties getting work. My first job was as a stock clerk." Although factors not related to race may explain his search difficulties, they occurred during a time that chemicals were a growth industry in the United States (Urban League 1961). His report is consistent with research indicating that blacks were underrepresented in the faster-growing industries in Chicago between 1950 and 1966, particularly trade, finance, insurance, and real estate (McKersie n.d.). Moreover, while his job opportunities in the white private sector were initially limited, the scope of his opportunities later broadened dramatically. After languishing in an entry-level technical job in a chemical company, he was recruited by a major clothier into a management trainee slot in 1967. In 1986 he was a vice-president and marketing manager in a major Chicago-based firm within the wholesale food industry.

A second college-educated man, a regional vice-president of sales for a major consumer goods company, also believed he experienced underemployment. After his graduation from a white midwestern college, he went to work in the marketing department of a large oil company. He reported, "I was supposed to be doing a lot of their market research and stuff like that. But I was just a clerk really, and there really wasn't much of a career opportunity." As he put it, "They would tell me, when openings came up, that, you know, their other [i.e., white] managers had to have those slots. So I just didn't see a future at [the company] being that I was black." In this case, also, perhaps he was limited not because he was black, but because of nonracial characteristics. If so, however, such characteristics did not preclude several major companies from offering him chances to enter management training positions after 1965. Moreover, he did not languish at the lower levels but moved rapidly up the job hierarchy once he went to work for his current employer.

Other illustrations of white-collar occupational segregation and truncated job opportunities come from college-educated blacks who entered sales fields in Chicago before the mid-1960s. In 1960, the median level of education for whites in sales was about twelve years;

three of the five executives I interviewed had a college education when they began their careers in sales before 1965.

In the late 1950s and early 1960s, consumer goods and wholesale trade companies adopted a marketing strategy in which they racially segmented sales areas into white and "special" markets known as "tan" territories. The terms are euphemisms for geographic areas dominated by black consumers. The practice of hiring blacks into predominantly white sales organizations and then steering them into black-oriented sales jobs was, and still is, common. A vice-president and regional sales manager for a Fortune 500 industrial said of his employer that "you would find that in Harlem and the Bronx, Brooklyn, you would basically have black sales reps, or Hispanic."

The first series of private sector jobs held by one man was limited to sales in black communities, although he had a bachelor's degree from a private white university. Between 1959 and 1964 he worked for a major alcohol beverage company and for a major tobacco company. Next, he found work in a black-owned hair care products company. It was not until 1968 that a white-owned company finally recruited him for a "crossover" job in general market (white) territories. This individual's career included time as a professional baseball player, and he described how routes into the white private sector were open only to a very limited group of blacks previous to anti-discrimination legislation. "Black [athletes] were the first in all of these [sales jobs], and we were selling to the black community. If you were a black athlete, then you had some high visibility and that generally was how you got into a major corporation."

Confining blacks to tan territories was a way for companies to better compete for the black consumer dollar without alienating white colleagues and customers. Although tan territories were the first markets that companies outside the South opened up to black salespeople, they did not offer jobs from which blacks would ordinarily move up in a company or get training in the merchandising business. Black territories were considered poor sales targets because the preponderance of black consumers had limited disposable income. The unanticipated consequence of such discriminatory marketing and employment policies was the discovery of the economic potential and the name-brand loyalty of the black community. Thus today, many companies aim different marketing strategies at black, white, Hispanic, and other special target groups. And companies have adopted some of the approaches developed for black consumers by black special market people to general markets and advertising (Davis and Watson 1982:18).

Professional Jobs and Government Contractors

Some of the people I spoke with did break into the professional mainstream in white companies before the 1960s. However, these opportunities were available only to those holding advanced degrees. Moreover, even within this educationally elite group, job opportunities suffered from racially based limitations. Almost exclusively, good job offers came from companies serving as federal contractors that therefore were sensitive to government oversight.

From the 1940s onward, the federal government stipulated that private industry receiving defense-related government contracts must address employment discrimination. One executive I interviewed had an MBA in finance from a relatively prestigious white university on the West Coast. He indicated that when he entered the labor force in 1962, federal government contract compliance laws induced large government contractors to hire highly educated blacks. And, indeed, between 1960 and 1966, blacks increased their employment in prominent companies in Chicago, most of them federal contractors with Plans for Progress (McKersie n.d.). While this seems like a positive reminiscence, he went on to say, "I wanted to be in the investment banking community, but there was no opportunity there at all. I finally settled on a job as an accountant at [an aerospace firm]. The [company] stacked the roster, they wanted lots of graduate degrees, and they wanted minorities, despite the fact that there were not the obvious or blatant kind of affirmative regulations [at that time]. And I was not doing work [at] the level of an MBA."

Although this executive was able to break into a traditionally closed profession, he also believed that he began his career as an overqualified but underutilized accountant. There may be some statistical support for his beliefs, since in 1960 only about 9 percent of all accountants and auditors had five or more years of college education. In 1986 he was the only black CEO of a major insurance company, a subsidiary of a Fortune 500 conglomerate.

A second example is striking because the man I interviewed was one of only a handful of blacks who had a graduate degree in engineering in 1960. In 1986, he was vice-president of operations for a large electronics and communications firm.

> I must have gone on forty-seven interviews. I heard that I was too old, I was too young, I was overqualified, I was underqualified. I was everything except the fact that nobody wanted a black engineer. So when I came to this [defense contractor], they were the first corporation that really offered me a job as a full-blown engineer. [However] I worried about where I could go [in the company]. There was one other black engineer in the whole corporation and he had been around a long time. This man had graduated from the University of Illinois with a mechanical engineering degree when blacks couldn't even eat on campus. And all he was was an assistant manager.

Government Employment

Fewer than half of the twenty-nine people I interviewed who entered the labor market before 1965 worked initially in the white private sector. This is consistent with the fact that government was a significant resource for black employment prior to the 1960s. In 1960, for example, just 13 percent of white managers, but 21 percent of black managers and administrators, worked in government (U.S. Bureau of the Census 1963). The proportion of black managers and officials was 62 percent greater than that of whites (U.S. Bureau of the Census 1963). Before the mid-1960s, then, these highly educated men found their jobs in government agencies, black businesses, and black nonprofit agencies. The experience of a vice-president for sales for a Fortune 500 retailer is typical of that era. He began his career as a caseworker for the Chicago Housing Authority; in 1986 he was one of the highest-ranking black executives in the United States.

> When I came out of the army, I made some inquiries into job possibilities prior to discharge. And, in fact, a whole group of us had sent out a number of resumés to companies. I was in an unusual outfit. It was [made up] mostly of college graduates. And, I guess of about 2,600 people in that [outfit] maybe 15 percent were black. We had sent out a number of resumés to corporations, to social work concerns, to foundations, to colleges. The responses we got [were] very interesting. The responses [that blacks] got from companies concerning management trainee positions were nonexistent, you know. White companies did not respond to black resumés. Or, they'd say that they didn't have anything open that you'd be interested in. It was interesting because there was a definite difference in the response of these companies between black and white resumés.

This man said that he came to the same conclusion "that educated blacks came to [then], and prior to that. The best opportunities [were] with governmental agencies and quasi-governmental agencies." When white corporations in the Midwest discouraged his application for management training jobs, this executive used his college degree to find a public sector job in social work. Five years later, in 1965, he was courted by a white company to enter management training.

His personal experience, and even his memory of these events, may be biased. However, others told similar tales about government employment. A director of affirmative action who worked for the same Midwest-based company said, "I was a teacher; my parents were teachers. At that time that's pretty much what you were going to do if you were able to go to college. You were going to be a teacher or a social worker." In 1961 she began working as a government employee; in 1966, she was recruited for a management training program in white private industry.

The hiring policies that excluded these people from good jobs in corporations in the Midwest also were reported by educated blacks who sought work in other parts of the country, although the prevalence of these conditions is not explicitly documented. For instance, a current vice-president of manufacturing who entered the labor market in 1964 in Arkansas noted:

> There were just not many opportunities. So, you catch the first thing you can get. And, at the time I was looking, they were just starting this [poverty] program. It had nothing to do with my background and nothing to do with my interests at the time. I had a degree in math, and I was looking to get into research. But, again, in that part of the country, and during those times, you either had to work for the government, or . . . that's it.

In 1966, he answered an advertisement in a white daily newspaper and found an entry level training position with his current employer, a company in the food-manufacturing industry.

In summary, before the mid-1960s corporate America made few professional and managerial jobs available to college-educated blacks, as the reports here reflect. After the mid-1960s, these people were in much greater demand in the private sector; they entered high-paying and prestigious jobs in white settings that had rigorously shunned them only a few years previously. Between 1950 and 1966 the occupational position of black compared to white men actually declined in Chicago (McKersie n.d.). But after the mid-1960s, at least for some better-educated blacks, the employment outlook changed dramatically. As one executive summarized it, "The same employment agency that turned me away in 1960 helped me find a job in the private sector in 1966."

Political Pressures on Private Employers

Despite their high levels of education, the people that I interviewed experienced their race before 1965 as a criterion for exclusion from good jobs in private industry. Further, data show that, given education and age qualifications, black men in Chicago faced somewhat more job exclusion than was generally the case for blacks in other central cities (McKersie n.d.). The Chicago experience illustrates the transcendent social fact of the time period, economic exclusion. After 1965, however, race became less of a barrier. Fifty-four of the seventy-six people I interviewed (71 percent) attributed this shift, at least in part, to the political pressures that shaped the 1960s and influenced this hiring period.

By the mid-1960s, federal employment legislation and an increasingly militant black community pressured the white business community to employ blacks. Grass-roots groups led by black ministers and other community leaders demanded that major employers start programs to expand black employment and business procurement opportunities (Cohn 1975). At the same time, urban rioting appeared to jeopardize not only the stores and plants but the sales markets of white businesses. Moreover, Title VII of the 1964 Civil Rights Act gave private citizens the right to sue over employment discrimination and made legal prohibitions against job discrimination enforceable for the first time in history (Hill 1977). In the 1960s, the federal government stipulated that major employers should correct employment inequality and by the early 1970s required federal contractors to submit affirmative action plans for hiring and promoting blacks and other specified minorities. The people I interviewed believe that new job opportunities emerged because of this federal affirmative action legislation and because of community-based political pressures, including urban violence.

Federal Legislation

By the time Title VII was enacted by Congress it had become increasingly evident that meaningful enforcement of a fair-employment law would require active federal intervention in hiring (Hill 1977). The premise of the law was that, based on past performance, major employers were likely to maintain the very barriers to equal employment opportunity that in the 1960s jeopardized the well-being of the entire nation (U.S. Commission on Civil Rights

1969). The employment protocol of the American Can Company in the 1960s illustrates the potential of Title VII to improve the socio-economic status of blacks through federal intervention. One facility of the company, which was a large federal contractor, drew its employees in 1969 from a rural area in Alabama where the population was about 57 percent black. Yet, the facility perpetuated racial inequality by employing blacks in just 7 percent (108) of its 1,550 jobs, and in only "several" skilled positions (U.S. Commission on Civil Rights 1969). The company also maintained other systems of inequality, such as owning a town in which totally segregated rental housing was maintained for company employees. In this town only 8 of the 123 company-owned houses that were rented to blacks had running water and indoor toilets. The contractor and subcontractor clause of Title VII enabled the government to intervene with the threat to withdraw federal contracts. As discussed in Chapter 2, the power of such a threat could alter exclusionary practices in this and similar employment settings. In 1969, an estimated one-third of the nation's labor force was employed by federal contractors, who made up a sizable proportion of the largest industrial employers (U.S. Commission on Civil Rights 1969). Accordingly, Title VII had the power to ameliorate a significant source of race-based social inequality.

The two categories of employers that fall within the regulatory sphere of Title VII are (1) companies with one hundred or more employees and federal contractors with fifty or more employees and (2) federal contractors or subcontractors selling goods or services worth at least $50,000. Consequently, large segments of corporate America came under pressure in the 1960s when they became targets of civil litigation and the courts ordered broad remedies when enforcing the central concepts of the law. In 1965, for instance, the Illinois Fair Employment Practices Commission ordered the Motorola Corporation to either stop employment testing altogether or replace their current biased test with one that was nondiscriminatory (Hill 1977). Although the monetary award for damages was eventually rescinded, the ruling received much publicity and set an important legal precedent (Hill 1977); indeed, employers' use of tests has been successfully challenged.[2] In 1966, in *Hall v. Werthan Bag Corp.* (251 F. Supp. 184, 186 [M.D. Tenn 1966]), the district court upheld the right to bring class action suits and thereby rejected efforts of employers to protect institutionalized forms of discrimination. In 1968, a federal district court held in *Quarles v. Philip Morris, Inc.* (279 F. Supp. 505 [E.D. Va. 1968]), that Philip Morris's assignment of black employees to departments with limited advancement potential was discriminatory. The court required the company to adopt a plan of interdepartmental transfer and promotion to eliminate this disadvantage.

Corporate America also came under pressure in the 1960s as the federal government's contract compliance programs increasingly held federal contractors accountable for following aggressive hiring plans, known as affirmative action. In 1967, the Office of Federal Contract Compliance (OFCC) began to impose affirmative-action standards on designated federal projects, such as the construction of the Bay Area Rapid Transit system in San Francisco (U.S. Commission on Civil Rights 1969). In 1969, the OFCC for the first time commenced proceedings to debar contractors for noncompliance (U.S. Commission on Civil Rights 1969). By the early 1970s, the federal government reached the apex of its commitment to implement programs to correct employment inequality. In 1970, Order No. 4 required contractors to set goals and timetables for hiring minorities. In 1972, Revised Order No. 4 specified in detail how contractors should comply with hiring obligations or face losing federal contracts. Major employers also came under investigation and litigation by the EEOC and settled job discrimination suits for millions of dollars in damages (Hill 1977; Lydenberg et al. 1986).

The judicial interpretations and enforcement of Title VII, the federal scrutiny of major employers, and the threat of losing sizable federal contracts all proved powerful incentives for corporations to correct longstanding employment inequalities (Ashenfelter and Heckman 1976; Freeman 1973; Leonard 1984; Vroman 1974). Spurred by them, the corporate world suddenly found ways to open job opportunities to a new echelon of skilled and educated blacks. For instance, the percentage of minorities among Philip Morris's officials and managers rose from no blacks in 1969 to 5.7 percent minority in 1972. In 1985, 15.4 percent of the company's officials and managers were minorities (Lydenberg et al. 1986).

In 1972, General Electric was among the first high-tech companies to create support programs to increase the numbers of minorities in engineering. General Electric also began a summer job-training program for minorities and funded minority scholarships at colleges and universities. Continental Bank in Chicago set up the Inroads program to provide summer jobs for black college students to familiarize them with the banking industry. A Northwestern student sponsored by the program became the first black in the bank's bond department, according to an article in the *Chicago Reporter* in May 1974, "Few in Top Jobs." The Chicago office of Arthur Andersen & Company, a Big 8 accounting firm, started recruiting at black universities in 1965; the Chicago office of Touche Ross first recruited at black schools in 1967, according to an October 1975 *Chicago Reporter* piece, "In the Red on Blacks." Three-quarters of the people I interviewed who entered managerial fields after 1965 (twenty-seven of thirty-six) reported that their employment was a result of a company effort designed to hire blacks. A senior investment analyst, whose first job in a white company was in the financial industry, describes his recruitment in 1972 this way:

> After they found out who I was they recruited me. I just happened to be out at [the company] and put in an application. Once they found out who I was they came after me. [Question: What do you mean by who you were?] Black. They saw I was black. They were looking for a black. They had put the word out in the [black] community. One of the people they had put the word out to in the black community was a person that I knew very well, and I had been listing that person as a reference on my applications.

One striking example of this flurry of recruitment came from a technical director of research for a Chicago communications company. He reported that in 1971, when he had just completed his doctorate in engineering, a major corporation was so interested in him that they not only offered him nine different jobs but even proposed sending him back to law school so he could work on their discrimination suits.

It was within this revolutionized hiring context that the employment opportunities of the executives I interviewed were greatly enhanced after 1965, reflecting the much broader market demand for black labor. Almost three-quarters of them (fifty-four of seventy-six) accepted their first job in the white private sector between 1965 and 1974, when federal implementation of Title VII was at its peak. A white supervisor at a large Chicago-based retailer told one executive with a college degree in education during his job interview, "We'd love to have your type." When I asked what he meant by "your type," the executive told me that, in 1972, "they needed a nigger. . . . They told me soon after I was hired that they were interested at that point in upping their numbers for the affirmative-action program. Because they had products that, if they were going to have to sell to the government, they had to have an affirmative-action program." After 1965, first jobs for these interviewees came much more often from the private sector than from government and black businesses. The rate of entry into the professional-managerial strata of private sector jobs also jumped dramatically. About twice as many post-1965 entrants as pre-1965 entrants had access to the white private sector via white-oriented supervisory, managerial, and management-training jobs.

During the 1960s and 1970s, these African Americans increasingly were hired into higher-paying and highly visible jobs that gave them authority in their interactions with whites. In the private sector, they were hired into sales tied to total consumer sectors, rather than to black sectors, and into management and trainee positions in which they supervised whites. An executive employed in the communications industry described the effect of government legislation on his personal mobility and the reduction of racial disparities in supervisory positions in his company. He explained that his transition into management in 1969 was, at least in part, a result of political pressure stemming from government affirmative-action legislation. He reported that the executive director of the company was strongly influenced by affirmative action. He told his department heads and directors, essentially, "We don't have any black supervision in this location. I want you to go out and, at your next opportunity, find a black who's qualified to be promoted to supervisor, and promote him." So somehow I was located in the company. I had done reasonably well, and they came down from [Columbus, Ohio] and interviewed me and offered me the supervisory job. I was promoted at a time the affirmative-action policies were really getting off the ground, and people were resisting that notion all across the company.

An impression reported by a second executive who is employed by a major food company is consistent with this theme. He, too, believes that he owes his transition into management to governmental pressures in the background. "In 1973, I think that their objective was to get a black in a management position and preferably to get one who was qualified. I think that was part of the project I was serving when I was promoted." Overall, these alterations in the pattern of black employment are substantively consistent with research based on aggregate data on black middle-class growth (Farley 1977; Freeman 1976a). The economic status of the black middle class rose as college-educated blacks were hired to fill new work roles. Government intervention via affirmative-action and contract compliance programs played a crucial role in advancing many of these individuals, and it did so by legitimating, not overriding, objective criteria that entitled blacks to equal employment.

The Rise of Black Militancy

The federal government was only one, albeit powerful, ally in blacks' struggle for more social and economic resources during this period. Preceded by a decade of black-white confrontations in the South, civil rights legislation was accompanied by the escalation of black activism and civil disorder in northern urban areas (Bloom 1987; Sitkoff 1981). The executives I interviewed believed that a combination of these escalating social factors also contributed to the expansion of their job opportunities, particularly in the 1960s. That these middle-class blacks consciously connected their gains to disruption in the lower classes points to a race-conscious connection among blacks that transcends class differences. Moreover, it differs from the response of the white middle class, which tended to distance itself from white political action groups such as the Students for a Democratic Society (SDS) and the Weathermen. Upon entering managerial fields in the white private sector, these black executives recognized that organized black boycotts and the ideological militancy of black organizations were instrumental in creating access to these jobs.

An example of this perspective comes from a manager of community affairs who told me that when black political organizations such as the Student Nonviolent Coordinating Committee (SNCC) were becoming more active in the North, his employer was unprepared, both culturally and administratively, to respond to approaches from these groups asking for jobs and contributions. In addition, this manager reported that the emergence of black militancy and the call for "black power" encouraged existing black staff in the company to coalesce and become increasingly insistent that the company demonstrate social sensitivity to the needs of the black community. As the manager summarized the late 1960s context:

> Those were things [that] were in the works at that time [and] the leadership of [the company] looks around here and it's all white men that you see. There wasn't a black face in any one of these [Chicago corporate] offices. They had a few blacks in some cubical . . . but no one that was to be a manager. So here was a tremendous opportunity to make this nigger a manager. [Question: This nigger? Do you mean you?] Sure.

In 1970, this man was the first black to be hired into the company's corporate offices with the title "manager"; he became the manager of community relations.

By the 1960s, blacks' campaign for equal rights was based on activist strategies reflecting the rise both of more aggressive black ideologies and of mass-based, grass-roots organizations (Bloom 1987). The narrow and more conservative, legalistic approach to winning racial equality taken by the National Association for the Advancement of Colored People (NAACP) during the 1940s and 1950s gave way to direct action and confrontational strategies by newer black organizations that reflected both the growing cohesiveness among blacks and the rise of black militancy.[3] In the South, changing attitudes helped in 1957 to create the Southern Christian Leadership Conference (SCLC) and, in 1960, the more militant SNCC. Based in the North, the Congress on Racial Equality (CORE) was known for its broad-based appeal to blacks and its unorthodox, militant methods of reform. These organizations used nonviolent and mass collective activities to disrupt the status quo and pressure white institutions they sought to change (Bloom 1987).

During the 1960s, protest demonstrations transcended issues relevant only to the South, and the movement focused on a broader range of economic issues (Bloom 1987; Newman et al. 1978). As militancy increased, black demands for better housing, education, and jobs spread across the entire nation.[4] And, as black protest shifted from the South to the North, sit-ins, shop-ins, and other forms of demonstration highlighted the need of blacks for broader economic opportunities. In the mid-1960s, for example, the NAACP started a nationwide campaign to open previously closed jobs to blacks, particularly higher-paying supervisory, professional, and managerial positions, and to admit blacks to specialized company training programs. CORE held demonstrations that, among other issues, pressed for black jobs in retail businesses, banks, and the construction industry (Bloom 1987:196). In short, blacks protested the unequal allocation of economic resources and demanded a black fair share of corporate contributions, jobs, and black-owned business procurement opportunities. The *Harvard Business Review* notes that Fortune 500 companies were now approached by the more militant minority-group organizations such as CORE, SNCC, and the Welfare Rights Organization (Cohn 1975:10).

Black Economic Boycotts

By the mid-1960s, southern business had already experienced the impact of boycotts in which black consumers withheld their patronage from white businesses (Bloom 1987). Given its success in the South, the use of black consumer power as a tool to negotiate for jobs and for black economic development in the North proliferated in the 1960s. In Chicago, for example, Jesse Jackson in 1967 organized Chicago's black ministers to support Operation Breadbasket, the economic arm of the SCLC, to find jobs for blacks in bakeries, milk companies, and other firms with products that had heavy black patronage (Colton 1989). In 1971, Jackson launched PUSH for the same purpose: to use black consumer power to increase the number of black jobs and black business procurement opportunities in white corporations (Jackson 1979).

Although the impact of black economic boycotts on the southern social structure is well documented (Bloom 1987; Sitkoff 1981), their effect on black jobs in the North appears not to be precisely known. However, economic boycotts by blacks arguably would provide enough motivation for companies to get involved in equal employment opportunity programs. Retail outlets and consumer goods manufacturers are particularly vulnerable to a black boycott of products (Haynes 1968). For example, a 1961 study by Roper and Associates commissioned by Pepsi-Cola found blacks drank more soft drinks than whites and were much more likely than whites to drink Coca-Cola. In response to this survey, Pepsi-Cola launched an advertising and public relations campaign to woo black consumers, which netted Pepsi-Cola almost $100 million in additional annual profit (Gibson 1978).

An argument for corporate responsiveness is also implied in the recollections of a black personnel director at a food manufacturer with high name-brand recognition. He noted that in the late 1960s there was an "extraordinary awareness on [his employer's] part that there was a black consumer market out there that [the company] needed to appeal to." During his tenure, he recalled, the company hired a black consulting firm that presented evidence to senior management of a large segment of black consumers who "never heard of mayonnaise, but who eat [brand name] like crazy . . . who have never heard of cheddar cheese, but eat [brand name] like crazy."[5] This man went on to say that, as a result of this heightened awareness of buying patterns, the company started a black marketing program. He said, "I hated that title, [but] that's what we called it at the time." The threat posed by economic boycotts is a consistent theme in the tales of corporate recruitment. A director of community affairs and district personnel manager described his management trainee position in 1966 as a response to Operation Breadbasket's threats of a black consumer boycott against a chain of food stores in Chicago: "The store had about 32 operations in the black community and nobody in management. They had a big black consumer base. So Jesse came in and got a [hiring] covenant. I got hired as a part of that covenant. Blacks started coming into the business structure at that time. I would say [the store] put at least twenty to twenty-five blacks into management training at that time."

A similar story was told by a man who had worked in the New York clothing industry. This vice-president, whose first job was assistant manager in a clothing store in 1966, was hired when the NAACP organized black consumers to take action against the retailer. Until that confrontation, he said, "it was well known in the black community that blacks could not get good jobs there," and blacks were absent within the management structure of the company. When he was hired, he explained, "managers were, you know, the guy would be the manager of the porters, or the elevator starters, or the kitchen. But there were no front-line blacks in buying or merchandising responsibilities. And black people spent a lot of money in [the store]. So that's how I got in — because of the pressures of the NAACP picketing."

A man who entered the white private sector in Ohio echoed his story. This director of human resources for sales operations explained that he was the first black college graduate recruited in 1967 as a management trainee in a Cincinnati-based consumer goods company because of the actions of the SCLC. Although his hire might have been merely a coincidence of timing, research indicates that black demonstrations against a single employer often prompted other employers to hire blacks as well (Meier 1967). He recalled, "Some of the companies were being boycotted . . . by SCLC and a coalition of ministers in the Cincinnati area. They had gone [after] companies like Kroger and Procter & Gamble and other highly visible consumer companies. Before they hired me there weren't any blacks and there wasn't a management training program. I was it."

By 1982, Jesse Jackson had signed more than a dozen moral (i.e., not legally binding) covenants with major corporations such as Coca-Cola, Seven-Up, and General Foods (Jackson 1979). Such willingness on the part of consumer goods companies to sign trade agreements, and the insights of the managers I interviewed, point to a sensitivity in the retail business to its market share and, therefore, its consumer base. In markets where blacks constituted a "sizable enough" proportion of sales, there is reason to believe that top management would respond to boycotts by increasing the number of blacks visible to consumers and upgrade some blacks to jobs in management. Of course, data on black employment comparing firms by the size and strength of their black consumer market would be necessary to support this point.

The Urban Crisis

Black urban unrest also appears to have helped motivate major employers to start programs to expand black job and economic opportunities. For example, one executive reported that his employer, a leading food company, faced tremendous pressure during the riots from black groups in different sectors of the country. Black organizations were demanding that the company create black ownership as the price of doing business in black communities. As a result, in 1968 the company set up an urban affairs program, headed by this executive, that generated two black-owned franchises in Chicago and one in Cleveland, firsts in the company's history.

Between 1965 and 1970 one-third of 247 urban-based Fortune 500 companies started programs that would expand black economic opportunities, "principally to help discourage boycotts, violence, and other threats to company well-being" (Cohn 1975). Piven and Cloward (1971) offer evidence that the private sector participated heavily in a strategy of appeasement by providing a multitude of services and technical assistance to black ghettos via community action, manpower-training grants, and urban redevelopment programs. To preserve a profit-making environment, U.S. businesses responded to the riots and the shock waves generated by the 1968 Kerner Commission's report by starting black economic development programs as one solution to the urban crisis (Cohn 1975; *Fortune* 1968; Henderson 1968).

The series of long hot summers of urban riots began in the mid-1960s and continued until the end of the decade.[6] With half of the black population in the United States compressed within the ghettos in large northern cities (Bloom 1987), private industry faced pressures in addition to those from federal legislation, potential profit loss, and bad public relations due to economic boycotts. The people I interviewed believed that companies also opened jobs in fear of the destruction of physical assets, such as company plants, located in or near volatile black neighborhoods. They attributed their enhanced opportunities for professional and managerial job opportunities during this time to the spiraling outbreaks of black riots in central cities. Two-thirds of thirty-five informants entering the white private sector after 1965 in managerial fields described their companies' vulnerability to black consumer boycotts and to urban upheaval. For example, a manager of community affairs for a public utility who was hired following riots in Chicago shared the following perspective:

> I'm not too sure that if we could we wouldn't [have taken] the cable out of the ground and off the poles [in] . . . north Lawndale which is black, and south Lawndale which is mainly Hispanic. Some of the employment programs [were] motivated [by] a desire to do good . . . but some of it was to develop good public relations as a buffer around the assets that the company has in [those neighborhoods].

Typically, literature on urban rioting looks at the relationship between racial insurgency and the expansion of social welfare and government programs for the black poor (Isaac and Kelly 1981; Piven and Cloward 1971, 1977). In contrast, my research suggests that riots helped to create white-collar jobs and economic programs for blacks in the private sector. Although a tendency exists to associate urban programs with the black disadvantaged and the hard-core unemployed, these programs just as often were outreach efforts by major employers to hire and economically upgrade a more advantaged black population. Urban-based Fortune 500 companies had more minority and urban affairs programs to recruit and train blacks who were both skilled and qualified to fill jobs than programs to employ or train the hard-core poor and unemployed (Cohn 1975:11): twenty-one companies made special efforts to recruit blacks directly into managerial and executive positions, while seventy-one others set up management-training programs for blacks already on the company payroll. In reaction to urban riots, companies in every industry group set up these new programs (Cohn 1975). A new corporate consciousness is also suggested in the account of a vice-president of sales who was the first black ever hired into management in a huge retail company. Significantly, he was hired in 1969, immediately following a period of rioting in East Cleveland during which a nearby competitor burned down: "Our store was not far from East Cleveland. All of a sudden headquarters called [and] said, 'We want you [for the management] job.' The store I was put in . . . was 50 percent black. So then it became very clear. [Question: That your employment was connected to the rioting?] That's right." (My question may seem to have loaded the answer, but by that point in the interview the man's condescension toward the actions of his employer had become quite apparent. I interpreted his truncated explanation as a shorthand used because he viewed me, a black woman, as an insider who would understand what he meant by "it became very clear.")

His interpretation is consistent with research reported in the *Harvard Business Review* (Cohn 1975). He viewed the increased black visibility in management as a public relations effort forced upon the company to stave off the destruction of its assets. It is also consistent with more recent observations of the effect of the 1993 Los

Angeles riots; this one from the *Los Angeles Times* is typical (Harris 1994):

> Two years ago, Joe Naphier, then a human resources manager on a McDonnell Douglas commercial airline project, stood on the executive floor with company President Robert Hood and watched Los Angeles burn. The two men talked. Two months later, Naphier, who had been with the company for 14 years and was then the only black general manager, was named to head a diversity committee. Four months later, he was promoted to ombudsman, a position last held by a company vice president. He got a nice raise as the first black face ever in that sensitive position . . . and has no problems telling you that the riots are the reason he's there. The paradox of riots emerges. Riots failed to benefit the social and economically disenfranchised, rather — in this instance at least — it helped a well-placed few.

Rioting has been interpreted as an attempt to draw attention to the needs of poor blacks, yet its result in the 1960s was the destruction of urban ghettos that never got rebuilt. Social policy responses to alleviate black upheaval in urban areas benefit blacks who were less, rather than more, impoverished by their environment — in this part of his argument Wilson (1978, 1981) is precisely right. For the poor, jobs are still hard to come by, the black family is still in trouble, and the life chances of residents of urban ghettos look dim and are darkening. The consequences of rioting seem much less ambiguous for the better-off, such as the group I interviewed. They are part of a new black middle class working in professional and managerial jobs once traditionally set aside for whites in private sector institutions.

It is interesting to recall, nevertheless, that middle-class blacks consciously connect their gains to disruption in the lower classes. A racial awareness exists within the middle class of a political connection that overrides some ideologies based on class divisions. Moreover, a deeper irony may be revealed over time. Various coalitions of middle-class blacks may, indeed, be self-serving, but blacks in the middle class are not necessarily a permanent, nor even the ultimate, beneficiary of this new social arrangement. Blacks benefited from a political climate and racially oriented policies that produced mechanisms (i.e., roles) to address black needs. Ultimately, however, these racially sensitive mandates alleviated political pressures on white corporations. Without such pressures, what will happen to these black personnel?

Chapter 5

Race Tracks and Mainstream Careers

✦ Tracking African American managers into racialized jobs was a strategy white companies developed during the 1960s and 1970s, when these executives' value became tinged with race-conscious political purposes. For example, ten of seventeen managers (59 percent) that I interviewed, all with highly technical skills as accountants, engineers, chemists, and so on, were asked to fill such jobs. Twenty-two of the forty-five people (49 percent) in my interview group who became affirmative-action and urban affairs managers started in line areas but were recruited for racialized jobs, twelve of them (55 percent) by senior level white management, usually either senior vice-presidents or chief executive officers. Nine (41 percent) turned down the first offer and were approached a second time by top management. Eleven (50 percent) were given salary increases, more prestigious job titles, and promises of future rewards. The push in companies to fill new administrative roles in employment and social policy areas cut across both personal preference and previous work experience. A midlevel manager in his forties comments: "It was during the early 1970s, and there weren't very many people around that could do anything for minorities. . . . I mean, . . . all the companies were really scrambling. All you saw was minorities functioning in [affirmative action and urban affairs] and it doesn't take much brain power to figure out that that's where most of us were going to end up." A white senior vice-president of human resources noted that top management deployed people from line jobs into affirmative-action jobs to signal the rank and file that the company was serious in its commitment. Transferring an experienced line manager into affirmative action increased the credibility of a collateral role and enhanced its effectiveness. From one perspective it would seem that employers either ignored these executives' education and experience or used it against them.

These executives are among those who rose to the top by managing affirmative-action, urban affairs, manpower-training, and technical assistance programs. Twenty-six of the seventy-six black managers I interviewed spent their entire careers in racialized jobs outside the corporate mainstream. Another twenty-five held one or more racialized jobs but eventually moved permanently into the mainstream. Only twenty-five had careers made up only of white corporate mainstream jobs.

This high concentration in racialized jobs is consistent with the notion of a politically mediated black middle class. It indicates the nature of pressures on corporations and shows the incentives for getting blacks into these areas. Conversely, this high concentration calls into question notions of a color-blind allocation of labor and of a color-blind market demand.

To obtain a rough comparative measure, I conducted an informal survey of top white executives by asking twenty CEOs of major Chicago companies if they ever held affirmative-action or urban affairs jobs. (I asked about these jobs specifically because they typify racialized jobs.) Some seemed startled by the question, and only one reported having worked in either area, a CEO whose tasks in urban affairs fell in a different category from those performed by my black interviewees. Although this man represented the company on several citywide committees to improve race relations, his job, unlike the black executives I interviewed, was a part-time and temporary assignment, not a full-time and permanent position. The results of my informal survey suggested that among the managerial elite in Chicago, blacks are likely to have held racialized jobs, but whites are not. Moreover, just 5.9 percent of 698 respondents to Korn/Ferry's (1986) survey of corporate vice-presidents, senior vice-presidents, executive vice-presidents, chief financial officers, and group vice-presidents held positions in personnel or public relations departments, where companies tend to house affirmative-action and urban affairs jobs. More typically, the track to top jobs in companies includes profit-oriented positions such as sales, operations, and, more recently, finance (Korn/Ferry 1990).

African Americans in Mainstream Careers

Mainstream careers are grounded entirely in jobs with goals oriented to general (i.e., predominantly white) constituencies, not jobs produced in response to black protest and subsequent social policy. The career of a forty-year-old vice-president and regional sales manager for a Fortune 500 company in the manufacturing and retail food industry illustrates a mainstream work history. The executive holds a two-year college degree in natural sciences. When he entered the private sector in 1960 as a market researcher for a Fortune 500 East Coast oil company, his job involved marketing to the total (predominantly white) consumer market, not to "special" (predominantly black) markets. In 1968, he accepted a position as a salesman with his current employer, and, even in the midst of the civil rights era, he was never assigned to a black territory. He moved up through the sales hierarchy from salesman to sales manager, zone manager, district manager, area manager, division manager, and, eventually, to his present job in the company. Throughout his ascent, he was never responsible for a predominantly black sales force or for strategic marketing to the black community when he managed geographical areas. His current employer once offered him an affirmative-action job in personnel, but he declined the offer because of negative experiences in a similar, but unpaid, role thrust upon him by his first employer. Moreover, he perceived affirmative-action jobs as lacking power in the company.

Another illustration of a mainstream career executive is a highly recruited woman with an MBA from the University of Chicago who was a vice-president of investor relations. She entered the white private sector in 1968 and worked her way up in banking through a series of financial assignments. In 1984, she was recruited for an assistant vice-president and director's position with a leading food manufacturer in Chicago where, she said, she "could be a part of the management team." In 1985, she again was recruited, this time by her final employer in the private sector, and became a full vice-president and company officer. By 1993, she had left there to start her own business. This woman was never asked to implement, nor did she ever manage, programs related to blacks. (I asked, for instance, if she had participated in any bank program designed to give financial advice to black organizations, if she had ever consulted primarily with black consumers or investors, or if she had administered any Small Business Administration minority business start-up programs sponsored by the bank during her tenure.)

Mainstream executive careers represent the affirmative-action ideal, as opportunities for talented blacks to compete for power and prestige in business bureaucracies. Yet mainstream African American executives stand out as the exceptions. How were they able to avoid racialized assignments? One explanation is that their employers viewed them as too well trained to shift out of the mainstream. The banking executive's MBA from a prestigious school undoubtedly made her a unique commodity in 1968 relative to other black job candidates. Yet level of education has not proven a good predictor of career track. Executives I interviewed at each level — bachelor's, master's, and doctoral — had at least a fifty-fifty chance of getting a racialized job.

Another possible scenario is that companies filled affirmative-action and urban affairs jobs on an ad hoc basis. That is, when the need to develop programs arose, a company first looked in-house for black candidates to fill those positions. Conversely, if racialized jobs were already filled, mainstream people were more likely to stay mainstream. Each of the three firms the MBA worked in had affirmative-action and urban affairs programs in place when she came on board. Ten of twenty-five in mainstream competition also reported such programs in place when they were hired. In addition, the vice-president and regional sales manager offered his opinion that no pressure was exerted on him to manage affirmative action because another black professional in the company subsequently agreed to take the offer.

However, blacks' ability to move up in the mainstream of a company did not mean their careers evolved free of the influences of job discrimination (see Fernandez 1981; Jones 1986). Nevertheless, these two African American executives and others who built mainstream careers were extremely successful relative to most African Americans (and most whites). Both the MBA and the vice-president and regional sales manager made six-figure salaries. Both were officers in their respective companies in the 1980s.

The African American Mobility Trap

Most of the executives I interviewed (51 of 76) moved into and stayed in, or moved through, racialized jobs that also created barriers to corporate mobility. For example, a 46-year-old man who I'll refer to as the frustrated manager was initially hired by a major steel company in the 1960s for a job administering a federally funded in-house program for disadvantaged youth. Funded by the U.S. Department of Labor, the program was designed to train, or retrain, predominantly black Chicago youth in skills that would qualify them to work in Chicago's white private sector. The frustrated manager, who was a social worker employed by the city of Chicago before he was hired by the steel company, said the company identified him as a candidate for this position through his work with inner-city youth and gang members. He recalled being told during the initial interview with the personnel manager that his active ties to Chicago's inner-city youth, and the implication these ties had for program development, was a key reason the company was interested in hiring him. His response: "I told [the personnel manager] that I don't want a nigger job and I don't want to be dead ended. That's the job I didn't take. But I saw some value in the manpower training because it was an inroad for minorities and females."

The frustrated manager defined a "nigger job" as corporate "positions preidentified for blacks only. Those jobs have high-ranking titles and are highly visible but do not have any power in a company. Those jobs are not with the mainstream of [a] company [so they] would [not] turn into any kind of career with the company. [In contrast] real jobs [were positions by which] good performers could rise [in a company]." In other words, people in "real jobs," but not "nigger jobs," performed valued corporate functions and were thereby able to move up the corporate ladder. This man seemed to be ambitious and intense; he punctuated his recollections about his job interview by pounding his fist on the boardroom table. He recounted his career with pride in his voice, but also a hint of ambivalence about how far he had been able to go. He believed that because manpower-training programs served the disadvantaged (i.e., black) population, they created a need for skilled black labor, which gave him a chance to move into the white private sector in an administrative slot and to develop, he said, a "different kind of work experience." But, although he was interested in the job, he negotiated, he said, "up front so that [the company] would not dead end" him. He did not want this to be one of those "jobs in companies [where blacks are left] to die on the vine."

He also observed that corporate jobs administering manpower-training programs, which sprang up in the wake of urban riots, were similar to the training programs themselves: Both were vehicles corporations used to bring blacks into the private work force. However, he took the job because he perceived it not as a dead-end position but as a valid step on a career path leading to personnel director. He aspired to a career in personnel over other functions such as production, because he believed that "black people [at that time] had no involvement in managing [other] parts of a corporation." He also said, "I'm a people person and I knew I wanted to be a director of personnel. This was a way to get there, [and] that was agreed upon in that interview with [the personnel manager]."

It is doubtful the personnel director of the steel company in this case seriously viewed the manpower-training job as a route to a director of personnel job. Although the company explicitly recruited this manager because of his networks in the black community, implicitly management may have chosen him because they needed to hire a black person. The company was based in a riot-torn community, and the manpower-training program was part of an effort to improve the company's poor record of employment and training of African Americans. According to this man the company at the time employed only one other black professional. Apparently no one on board would, or in the company's judgment could, fill the position of manpower program director.

After the frustrated manager had the manpower-training program for two years, "very successfully," the company created a job for him as a community relations representative, part of a move "to institutionalize the [minority] manpower-training program within the organization" after federal funding ended. Two and a half years later, he moved into a second newly created job, community relations director, a promotion in both title and salary. Still proudly, he attributed his career mobility to his success in employing residents from the surrounding black community.

Although, according to the frustrated manager, the company was willing to promote him and increase his salary because he was meeting a need, his promotion did not move him into a mainstream personnel career. When asked what his last promotion meant in light of his original career goals, he admitted he was aware, even then, that his future in the company might be limited. "You have a little stepladder . . . a logical progression [of positions] you have to go through if you are to ever become a personnel director. I wasn't doing any of that. As far as I could see, the company wanted black folks to be my only responsibility." The manager reminded his superiors that his career goals lay elsewhere, but he was not deployed into mainstream personnel. He therefore viewed his movement within the company as promotions "in place," evidence that he "was not really experiencing mobility in [the corporate] structure." He also believed his ability to accomplish the job he was in was limited because of conflicts with the personnel director. He said, "My problem [in developing a good minority recruitment program] was not one of identifying qualified minorities, but of stopping discrimination among those with authority." An important part of his job, he pointed out, was to identify, and attempt to correct, irregular hiring patterns for which the regional director of personnel was ultimately responsible. "[Whites] were hired . . . who did not have high school diplomas, who could not speak English [and] could not pass any of those battery of tests that they give to the blacks or the women." When the program to improve minority hiring "worked out well, [the director of personnel] was the person who was embarrassed. He was the person who was made to change."

Believing his in-house options were limited, the frustrated manager volunteered to be a loaned executive on a citywide corporate project engaged in community and economic development. He felt this route "represented more training and [potential] mobility." In the early 1970s, after leading seminars on community relations for the steel company, he was courted for a personnel job in ten other companies. He decided to start over with a new computer firm and try, once again, for a director position. Yet, ironically, "community work" was involved even in his subsequent jobs in the computer field because those companies also were "not doing well in the recruitment of minorities."

I was unable to reinterview this man in 1992. However, the person who originally referred him to me reported that he had been transferred to California, was "still doing community affairs, and was ready for an early retirement." Secondhand reports are often suspect, but the two are friends, work for the same company, and talk with one another often. Our mutual acquaintance also said that their recent conversations about their current careers increasingly focus on personal disappointment and missed opportunities.

The frustrated manager, like one-third of the executives I interviewed, gained status in the private sector by filling corporate positions linked to black constituencies. At the same time, filling race-based roles effectively locked him out of conventional routes up the corporate ladder. Several facets of his career in the steel company converged to keep him out of the mainstream. First, he performed well in a position that, at that time, was valued in the company. Top management rewarded him with higher salaries and kept him assigned to that area. Consequently, he was excluded from experiences that would broaden his mastery of more generalized personnel functions. The lack of generalized experiences further undermined the legitimacy of his claims for promotion to a mainstream personnel job. Moreover, when he identified hiring biases in the company, intentionally or not, he criticized and alienated an important potential mentor, the regional personnel director. Finally, if he habitually used the word "nigger" in a conservative corporate environment it may have further minimized his chances for promotion. The provocative nature of that racial epithet could cause his image in the company to suffer and increase his chances of being left behind. He used the word often during our interview, and I wondered at the time if he used it with the personnel director.

Career-Enhancing Strategies

During the 1960s and 1970s, the executives studied here either began their careers in mainstream jobs or wanted to exchange racialized jobs for mainstream assignments. About half who wanted to move into the mainstream (25 of 51) achieved their goal. By 1986, executives who had left racialized areas had been out about nine years on average. They were distinguished from those who remained in racialized jobs by falling into one of two categories. One group was able to decipher the rules of the game by seeking mentors and other sources of information about meaningful career routes. They used that knowledge to generate career-enhancing moves, which included requesting alternative assignments. In the second category are workers for whom racialized jobs inadvertently became a career springboard toward solid — mainstream — ground.

Reading the System

Fourteen of the twenty-five who escaped the racialized sphere during the 1960s and 1970s simply asked to be reassigned. In contrast, only seven of the twenty-six who stayed in racialized jobs during this time asked to be reassigned. Virtually all who requested reassignment perceived both the trend in corporations to have black managers fill affirmative-action and urban affairs jobs and their potential to limit opportunities in the long run of corporate life. The group's collective consciousness is summed up in an observation about people who turn this type of job, made by a vice-president at a major electronics firm. This man started one affirmative-action program for a company and turned down several similar job offers from other companies. Referring to his stint in affirmative action, he said: "They would send me to some of these conferences [and] . . . you'd walk in and there would be a room full of blacks. . . . And I met titles, . . . directors and you name it, of equal employment opportunity. It was a terrible misuse at that time of some black talent. There were some black people in those jobs that were rather skilled, much like myself."

He recognized such job ghettoization as a race-related mobility trap for black managers. "During the 1960s and 1970s blacks in these jobs had fancy titles, but basically they were in dead-end positions," he said. Black executives approached to take such jobs faced a career dilemma. They believed they had to be committed team players to get ahead in the company, and at the same time they feared that if they succeeded in affirmative action or urban affairs, top management might never transfer them.

A forty-six-year-old sales vice-president expressed the first side of the dilemma when he explained, "In this company you don't turn down requests when they come from a senior vice-president, and especially when they look like a promotion." When he was asked to fill affirmative-action positions, however, he said he also "just wanted it to be up front" that he "didn't intend to keep that job forever," that he thought it necessary to set time limits on his transfer. Expressing the second side of the dilemma, he said, "You can do those [affirmative-action] jobs too well [or top management feels] . . . this is where you need to be." The sales vice-president mentioned earlier concurred with this observation. "All we had to do was to look at blacks around us to come to that conclusion."

Although they risked appearing recalcitrant, managers headed for mainstream careers stipulated time limits when taking racialized jobs and, once in these jobs, assertively requested reassignment. Many were eventually mainstreamed. The sales vice-president, for instance, transferred into an affirmative-action job from floor sales, but also set the stage for his mainstream reentry by negotiating a one-year limit on this placement before accepting the position. The company honored its promise and moved him out of affirmative action and into a buyer's position.

A current vice-president of human resources for a clothing manufacturer also requested a transfer from affirmative action because he recognized the limits of the job. This man transferred into affirmative action in 1967 when he worked for a federal contractor-operator of a huge munitions plant in southern Indiana. Although he was trained in and working as a research chemist, the personnel director approached him about transferring to personnel. He was the only black professional in an operating environment that was facing intense federal scrutiny. At the time he was approached, "the federal government had the big push on government contractors to do more for affirmative action," he explained. The plant was particularly vulnerable because it was wholly supported by millions of dollars in federal contracts. "A lot of the federal investigators were black," he observed, "and . . . so if anybody had a chance of staving off all kinds of repercussions, then a black probably had a better chance."

The job came with a salary this manager characterized as "a pretty good deal." Yet he agonized over taking the offer because he would be leaving "the laboratory," he said, for a job he "wasn't trained for."

To his surprise, personnel proved to be his true niche, and he went on to develop the plant's first affirmative-action program. But in 1970, he was worried about the vulnerability of his career track. He reasoned that affirmative action, as a field, was transient and did not offer technical skills that would allow him to branch out in a company. Affirmative action "is the kind of field where . . . a few laws might change, but the concept doesn't. Once you know those [laws], there's not an awful lot more to learn." Like the frustrated steel company manager, he realized that this avenue could diminish his ability to manage non-race-related personnel areas.

He also expressed the dilemma of becoming too successful. "My biggest concern was I was going to end up becoming the guy who handles all the EEO problems in the corporation. I'm thinking, [even] back in the early 1970s, . . . that if something ever happened to affirmative action, where it wasn't popular anymore, I wouldn't have any other marketable skills." Consequently, in 1972 he asked for, and moved laterally into, the mainstream job of personnel manager.

Twelve of the fourteen executives who asked to be reassigned to nonracialized positions pointed to the role of mentors and, more significantly, to their own fact-finding efforts as fundamental elements of their eventual transition into mainstream jobs. Those who stayed in racialized jobs read the business environment narrowly by observing blacks around them. But those who exited these jobs were more cognizant of the overall structure of a particular corporate hierarchy. They educated themselves, or found mentors, and assessed the corporate environment early in their careers, which enabled them to identify career-enhancing moves in their firm. For instance, a vice-president in a communications firm said that two years into his job, he knew "you can spend all the time you want . . . in personnel, and public relations, and that kind of stuff. But you aren't going to be a vice-president of this company, or president of this company without [going through] operations." Seventeen of twenty-five people who left racialized jobs specifically analyzed which routes led to the executive suites in their company. A vice-president in the communications industry told me, with a hint of condescension at having to state what to him appeared obvious, "All you had to do was look at who ran the company and see what areas they came from. I just observed who was sitting where. I looked at those yellow bulletins because they announced organization changes and because they also give personal bios."

Using Racialized Jobs as Springboards to the Mainstream

Executives I interviewed who had turned functionally segregated assignments to their advantage often found senior management mentors who trained and propelled them into core corporate positions. A vice-president of operations who has done postgraduate work in physics and engineering, for example, between 1968 and 1972 was an equal employment opportunity manager. The employee relations director at his first firm approached him to set up the company's affirmative-action program. He had been with the company eight years and, he said, "I wanted to get into management. That was the first and only opportunity that I felt I was going to get."

He said he believes he was approached for this role because "there was some concern that if you put the wrong guy in there that he would just raise all kinds of hell. And what safer guy could you get than someone who's sitting in the engineering department?" (Also, the company had only one or two blacks in professional jobs, and none in personnel.)

The company may have chosen this man merely because he seemed to have the requisite interests. During his off-hours he volunteered with black community agencies and often attempted to convince the company to donate funds to community projects in black areas. The firm, an aerospace company that subsisted on federal contracts, was extremely vulnerable to federal oversight. But in 1968, when the federal government's approach to contract compliance was relatively untested, the company was still unclear about affirmative-action mandates and its own direction in developing programs. As this executive put it, "Nobody knew how to do it, but everybody knew it would have to be good."

The company's dependence on federal contracts and its consequent emphasis on compliance with affirmative action made his job highly valued and anointed him with a status he knew no other black in the company had. He received "a job with a manager title, exposure to the company's inner works, and visibility to the corporation's top people." Yet he approached the job as if it were a steppingstone rather than a permanent stopping place — a chance, as he put it, to "let me get my nose somewhere" and "to get something for myself." As he developed the affirmative-action program in conjunction with a senior vice-president in the company, he did get something for himself — a powerful and active mentor. Up to that point, he said, "essentially I lacked what most blacks lack . . . sponsorship. I was totally on my own." He credited the sponsorship of this executive vice-president with his ability to turn his career around. "He was a white guy who . . . got to know me. Supported a lot of things that I wanted to do. And said, 'You know you've got a lot of capability, and it's a waste to keep you here in EEO. So I want to send you back to [Massachusetts Institute of Technology] because I think when you come back we can get you ready for a senior management job.'"

After administering affirmative action for five years, this man entered MIT's Sloan School of Management executive-training program. Soon afterward his mentor retired. When he returned from MIT, he expected the company to reward his achievements. "I was looking for a position where I could eventually do something, where I had some power." But offers for that type of position were not forthcoming. "I had forgotten I was black." Moreover, his mentor's protection and advocacy were gone. Despite his postgraduate work and success as an MIT-Sloan executive fellow, the offers that he received from his employer and, he stressed, from "so many other companies were to direct affirmative-action programs."

He said he heard about "all those guys I'd been with [at Sloan], . . . and their promotions." He believed that, at minimum, he should have been promoted to company director. After a lengthy pause, he said "[I] was screaming inside my head; I was hurt terribly by the [job offers]." But in spite of his initial disappointment, the training at Sloan (and, I would argue, the existence of federal anti-bias legislation) helped him to redirect his career. He told his employer, "No, hell no," he said. "I wouldn't even be interested in a job making decisions between black and white cars, let alone black and white people. I'm through with that. I've done my share." He demanded a line job, he said, because he "was no longer so naive to be seduced by title or salary." He subsequently became a project manager in his original company, staying with the firm for the next two years.

There is more bad news, however, and it is grounded in a by-now-familiar dilemma. In his efforts to achieve affirmative action as the company's EEO manager, the interviewee had alienated the man who later stepped into the executive vice-president position vacated by his mentor; he had "embarrassed" this person and "shoved something" he did not want "down his throat," he said. When he became a project manager, this adversary became his direct supervisor. His opportunities within the company stagnated once again.

One way to interpret the careers discussed thus far is to view them as blacks' struggles to succeed in a world where they are anomalies. In this context, blacks' unique status worked both for these people and against them. They were approached for racialized jobs because their visibility brought them to the attention of senior management. Such jobs were both potential springboards for, and hazards to, entering mainstream corporate training and competition. With an eye on both factors, they negotiated conditions for taking affirmative-action and urban affairs positions. In the case of the MIT-Sloan graduate, the racialized job was the vehicle that gave him a new chance — a mentor — and the year of additional specialized and prestigious training. Yet playing racialized roles also pigeonholed this man, inviting new affirmative-action job offers, creating a powerful enemy, and robbing him of a new mentor. Ultimately, however, occupying a racialized job created a window of opportunity, which this man used well. He eventually got other offers and went on to become a vice-president in a major firm.

In his first jobs, from 1963 to 1968, a vice-president and central region manager in a consumer goods industry he developed special markets successfully for two Chicago companies.

Although these special markets directly addressed each firm's economic initiatives, they were not a springboard from which blacks were expected to gain organizational power. Nevertheless, by 1968 this man's outstanding sales and performance records prompted senior management to create a new position for him as a special-market sales manager. His upgrade, while earned, was considered a radical innovation for this employer. His new position made him the second black manager in the company; the black executive who predated him ran urban affairs. He said that during this time, "I always wanted to break into the mainstream market but . . . I didn't even try. I just tried to do the best I could in that particular area." In 1973, five years after becoming special-market manager, his aspirations to participate in the mainstream came to fruition when the vice-president of sales promoted him to central division manager. From that point on, he moved quickly and steadily up the mainstream corporate ladder.

When asked what he thought influenced his ability to enlarge his racialized career, he recalled learning "a host of bottom-line functions" that eventually led him out of special markets. "I thought it was positive," he said. "It allowed me to learn the business — distribution, pricing, taxation, expenditures, promotional activities." His optimistic view of his opportunities, however, obscures the hiring discrimination that influenced his assignment to sales territories dominated by black consumers. He gives his early placement the gloss of an apprenticeship when he would have received similar — or possibly broader and better — training had he been given general-market assignments. But he was making his assessment based on what was possible for him at the time. When he was hired by this Chicago company, white companies simply did not offer blacks sales jobs in white-dominated geographic areas.

On the other hand, unlike the case of the frustrated manager in the steel industry, the same vision and skills this man demonstrated in special markets were recognized as valuable to the broader, mainstream sales territory. Although the timing of his recognition may have been an effect of governmental activity or some other race-related corporate considerations, his special-market assignment spotlighted his performance and prompted upper management to risk moving a black employee into a traditional (white) sales area. As he put it, "The vice-president of sales felt that I was good enough. He brought me in and really started teaching me the business."

The career path of a finance company's senior vice-president is a third example of converting a racialized job into a mainstream trajectory leading up the corporate hierarchy. In 1970, this man was transferred out of an entry level position and into a management role in the company's guaranteed loan program designed to assist small and minority businesses. The position had many pitfalls because it involved screening and lending capital to the most difficult, and economically vulnerable, customer base — owners of small black businesses. Thus when this manager generated profits, his success was both surprising and noteworthy. "We pulled it off," he said. "We made some good loans, and some folks became quite wealthy because of [them]. We had some real winners. We were doing so well that we got a pretty good reputation." As a result of his performance in lending, he was promoted into a commercial area he characterized as a "big hitter" and "for whites only."

When asked to give some background on this promotion, he said he viewed it as a natural progression in line with the job he had. His response assumes that his performance running the loan program created the perception among top management that he had the necessary skills to fill the higher position. Significantly, at about this time, a higher-placed executive took an interest in him and eventually became his lifelong mentor. In a tangible way, his racialized job in a profit-generating area gained him visibility and recognition that led to a permanent position in a formerly all-white domain.

Both this man and the special-markets manager discussed earlier became the first black members of all-white senior management teams. In both cases, their initial, and racialized, assignments became launching pads for mainstream careers. This man's client and business skills were perceived by top management as transferable to and, more important, better exploited in a mainstream profit-driven area. In addition, each had a mentor who played a crucial and active role in his ascent. Also, both mentors stepped forward after the workers excelled despite the limitations perceived to be inherent in their racialized assignments.

Golden Handcuffs and Social Obligations

Like the frustrated manager in the steel company, eighteen of the twenty-six workers who stayed in racialized jobs during the 1960s and 1970s aspired to mainstream positions at varying points in their private sector careers. Why, then, did only seven of the twenty-six request reassignment into core corporate functions? One theme among people who stayed in racialized jobs was that their ambitions were shaped, and sometimes thwarted, by their racial identity and a sense of racial solidarity. A second theme was that their ambition, compounded by their lack of practical knowledge about constructing corporate careers, made them easily seduced by racialized jobs and the corporate perquisites that often accompanied them. One manager who worked in sales before he took on affirmative-action responsibilities reminisced in a voice filled with irony that the move "was supposed to be an honor."

Individual Activism and Group Commitment

Racialized jobs struck a familiar chord with the executives who stayed in them, because they addressed social and political issues that permeated blacks' existence. The problems of black people were problems these men and women both lived and intellectually understood. Most were part of the first wave of blacks in the white private sector to benefit from civil rights pressures. They acknowledged their debt to the decades of struggle and expressed a strong obligation to "give something back" to the black community. Thus, when offered a job intended to assist blacks, some welcomed the jobs as their chance to help channel previously withheld resources such as jobs and contracts back into the black community. Once harnessed to the job by a commitment that linked their sense of group obligation with the administrative interests of a company, they became pigeonholed and entrenched in a racialized area. The recollections of a fifty-five-year-old director of affirmative action reflect this dilemma.

He began his private sector career in catalog operations management for a retail company in the mid-1960s. In 1969, in response to his complaints about the lack of management opportunities for blacks in the firm, the CEO asked him to set up the equal employment opportunity section. In 1992, he was still head of affirmative action for his third employer. Noting the disparity between where his career started and where it had gone, I asked him why he did not move back into a mainstream function. He mentioned a variety of factors.

I was trained for the operations end of the business but stayed in the [affirmative-action] end because I felt . . . I had an obligation to do something [for other black people] about that time, you know. Prior to that I really wasn't doing anything other than helping myself. But then in the 1960s people became really motivated . . . "black is beautiful" and the whole concept. And [the job] provided me with an opportunity to make a social contribution and also to continue to be successful in business.

At that time, he idealistically viewed affirmative action as beneficial to the business world because it changed the business environment. He also viewed it as a business contribution that generated resources and opportunities for less-advantaged black people. With pride he recalled that he was a member of one of the first Chicago coalitions to aggressively "address the issue of hardcore unemployment." He also offered what he considered a critical distinction between his generation of black managers and the succeeding generations of black business people: The new black managers "do not have the same sense of social responsibility that we had, . . . [they don't feel] an obligation to those back home" — that is, to other black people.

Paradoxically, he also believes that taking on the affirmative-action position was a misstep in his career. "If I had to go back and do it all over again," he said, "I would not stay in affirmative action. Them that brings in the dollars is where the most opportunity is. I advise my sons, . . . stay out of the staff functions, although those functions are very necessary." He went on to name people who took different routes, whom he views as "making it."

This manager's dilemma raises the question of whether, in the context of white corporate culture, some blacks' sense of group solidarity and responsibility worked against their own aspirations and mainstream development. Indeed, those who did permanently transfer out of racialized areas viewed such jobs as stigmatized in the corporate culture. Moreover, to hasten their departures, some quickly pawned their jobs off on black replacements who, they said, "cared more," or who had "closer ties to the black community."

Others who stayed in racialized jobs explicitly commented on the trade-offs they made between individual aspirations and community commitment in accepting racialized jobs. The case of a forty-five-year-old director of an urban investment program for a major consumer company provides one illustration. Before entering the private sector, this man spent a brief period as a professional basketball player and learned that he enjoyed interacting with people. Consequently, when he was hired in the early 1970s by a large insurance agency he requested a position in personnel. From that point his jobs and experiences evolved smoothly in mainstream personnel functions, and he let it be known that his eventual goal was to become a regional personnel vice-president.

Several years had passed when a senior vice-president in the company offered him a position as division personnel manager. Although the title does not signal a racial component, the job was, in fact, a specialty position focusing on strengthening the company's affirmative-action program. Like the frustrated manager in the steel company, this man knew that to progress up the corporate ladder in personnel, he needed to remain in and successfully carry out a series of mainstream functions. However, he took the racialized job offer: "I felt that if I had to make a choice, affirmative action for me was the most important thing. Because the rest [of the company's personnel functions] were going to take care of themselves." He subsequently moved in and out of racialized positions and occupied one when I first interviewed him. In his attempt to balance his community commitment and his career goals he repeatedly made career decisions he knew worked against his career interests. He knew, he said, that "people would perceive me as someone who was not being developed," and that, while he deeply desired it, he "probably would never become a regional vice-president." After a brief pause, he added, "Because I'm black, the company did probably use me to a certain extent." Yet after he made that comment, his race consciousness seemed to lead him to a different and intriguing conclusion: "But I didn't . . . mind using myself, if I could get more . . . black folks into the company. So it's hard for me to know what the truth is. Who's using who, and how much?"

He wasn't alone in his thinking. Fifteen of twenty-five executives who stayed in racialized areas also mentioned their sense of obligation to use their presence in the company to make a difference and to give something back to the black community. For example, an urban affairs director explained that staying in his job was his duty and his "way of civil righting back then." A director of corporate contributions explained his position by saying that "community affairs had been done in a little different way . . . by two other people who were white community-activist types. They were doing the job as agents of the company. And, while I'm sure people would say that I was doing the same thing, I didn't see it that way. I saw it more as the other direction. And [I think that I made] some breakthroughs in that area." A manager of government affairs noted, "We had a small group of about eight of us that met. We were all community relations managers for major companies. . . . We'd meet informally for lunch because we felt that our role was to facilitate some progress in the community and we couldn't do that if we didn't talk together and make a solid front."

Golden Handcuffs

But while a commitment to racial group solidarity was one motivation to stay in racialized jobs, less altruistic and more materialistic incentives to stay existed as well. *Golden handcuffs* refers to situations in which persons cannot take advantage of alternative opportunities because the cost of lost benefits would be too high. The power of golden handcuffs was summed up by a consultant who in 1968 moved into affirmative action from his job in accounting. "I sent the company signals," he said. . . . "I wanted to go back [into accounting] . . . but they do what it takes to keep you satisfied, salary increases and what not. So I stayed with this job." In other words, the material and psychic rewards associated with these jobs eventually proved to be traps.

Those in racialized jobs were greatly rewarded because they handled new and unpredictable contingencies facing companies. For example, more than 80 percent of first racialized jobs were created when these people filled them. Because these functions were new, top management looked to them for guidance and direction in shaping these areas. In turn, the ability to provide guidance gave these managers a unique status in companies. Managers who filled these jobs were on a first-name basis with corporate CEOs as well as with black nationalists from the streets, and their ability to walk between these conflicting groups made some of them favorite sons in corporations in the civil rights era.

In contrast to those who left racialized jobs, perceiving them as a barrier to their quest for assimilation, people who stayed in racialized jobs perceived them as their chance to become key players in shaping the goals of mainstream corporate life. It is a view similar to that held by the vice-president in the electronics firm when he described the EEO job as his chance to make it in the company and become a manager. The distinction, however, is that he saw the job as a stepping-stone; people who stayed in racialized jobs perceived them as powerful.

Among these was a fifty-two-year-old man who in 1986 worked for the same private sector employer that recruited him from his job at the Urban League in 1967. In both his first job as manpower coordinator and the job as district personnel manager that he held when I initially interviewed him, his function in the company was, he said, "always something relating to the black community." He "examined issues in the community," was "used as a negotiator," and generally "fixed problems with blacks" whenever they existed. Initially, these assignments fit in well with the overall direction he had envisioned for his career.

> My experience, both professional and in life, prepared me for that role in the company. That's what I do best. And I don't want to, didn't expect to, do anything more. The way I cajole myself, perhaps, is that somebody was going to do that job. And I felt that I would do that job with a sense of the community in mind. Not just because it would be a good job to earn money, and get you in and among people of ilk. Although it does. [Question: What do you mean by people of ilk?] I'm talking about people with money, and influence, and class.

He then paused and chuckled, as if reflecting on other incentives that influenced his career deliberations. Perhaps he was struck, as I was, by his use of the term "cajole" as an apparent synonym for "fool" and wondered if altruism was the only motivation shaping his decisions. His next comment revealed an equally significant reason he agreed to take the role.

> I made more money than I had ever dreamed of. Ordinarily, . . . I probably wouldn't have very much to do with people of ilk. [Not] if I was in some other kind of job. . . . Socially, that is not my place. You see, I represent a billion-dollar business here when I'm out there. And [there are] . . . not many places out there that are not open . . . to me. And that was one of the things that I discovered here. That's why I stayed.

Others echoed his sentiments, saying they stayed in racialized jobs in part because of their perceived benefits. During the 1960s and 1970s, they viewed such jobs as offering faster advancement, greater freedom and authority, and higher visibility and access to white corporate power brokers than the mainstream jobs of their black contemporaries. This new and distinctive social status also gave them an aura of power and prestige in the eyes of their black peers.

When I asked the affirmative-action director who advised his sons to stay out of staff functions if he ever tried to move back into the mainstream after he took on equal employment opportunity functions, to my surprise he said that he turned down a buyer's job offered to him by a vice-president in merchandising with his first employer. "I was stubborn at that point," he said. "No, I didn't want that." Given that buyers were key people in that organization and that the job was a stepping-stone to higher-paying positions, his refusal signals the attractiveness of racialized positions in companies during the civil rights era.

> Remember now, this [equal opportunity] stuff was exciting and there's a trap that you get into. Those of us who are in this kind of area talk about it all the time. It's kind of a golden handcuffs trap. We used to go on the convention circuit around the country . . . the Urban League and the NAACP, promoting our individual corporations. We were visible. We were representing the

company. We had big budgets. I mean, you know, you go to
every convention. And [you can] get yourself two or three suites
and entertain all the delegates. You could spend $15,000 or
$20,000 at a convention. I never had that kind of money to
spend, to sign a check, so it was very attractive.

To fully appreciate this manager's perspective, we should also
remember that the economic rewards and social status that accompanied racialized positions were unimaginable luxuries to most
blacks — in this or any employment sector — in the years preceding
federal fair employment legislation. Those who stayed in racialized
jobs were ambitious men who saw themselves doing the best they
could, given the limited job possibilities blacks historically had in
white companies. They weighed the jobs' perquisites against the
career stagnation common among the handful of blacks who had
previously attained management roles and remained trapped in low-
level positions.

In the 1960s and 1970s, these people thought racialized jobs were
their best opportunities for social and economic advancement. As a
fifty-three-year-old director of corporate contributions, then in his
twenty-third year in a racialized job, told me, "That was the place
for us to be." Many now see the downside of that decision. With the
benefit of hindsight, the affirmative-action director explained, "I
believe that had I stayed in operations [I would have] continued to
move up, and that's where the clout is. But the opportunity just
wasn't there [for blacks] when I first started with that company."
After a slight pause he added, somewhat ruefully, "Things changed,
and it is now."

Comments on Mentorship and Role Models

Role models and mentors may have changed the course of these
men's careers. The white corporate milieu and collegial relationships
with whites were new and mysterious to many people I interviewed.
Only twenty-six of seventy-six came from families where at least one
parent was a professional, managerial, or sales person. Moreover,

only two of the twenty-six had a parent, close relative, or friend who had professional work experience in a major corporation. Half had graduated from all-black colleges or universities. Since these executives, like most blacks, had not been exposed to the white corporate world, they had no one to help them decipher the rules of the game. Thus, historical restrictions on blacks' access to white corporate culture played a role in shaping their managerial career preferences.

Those who stayed in racialized jobs were as ambitious as those who got out of them; indeed — and ironically — ambition was a large part of the reason they stayed where they were. During the civil rights era, racialized jobs made educated, ambitious blacks company stars. Paradoxically, the most attractive features of the jobs, such as starting titles and salary, freedom, and visibility, for some of them also diluted their desire to move into the companies' mainstream areas. But with black role models, aggressive mentors, or more knowledge about company hierarchies, would those who stayed have made different career choices? Did they need mentors and role models to perceive alternative career options as truly possible? The district personnel manager who spoke of representing a billion-dollar business may, in retrospect, be satisfied with his career choices, but he now also understands that visibility among white business elites was not the same as power. The longtime affirmative-action manager now knows that, for corporate success in the long run, social commitment must come second to business decisions, important only when they support a company's profit-generating function.

When confronted with racialized job offers, these executives lacked the experience, role models, and mentorship to assist them in reading company culture. And, in the absence of support, blacks who remained in racialized jobs in Chicago corporations turned to each other for help in making career decisions. The affirmative-action director said, "It was a case of the blind leading the blind. I was stupid. I remember the CEO saying . . . 'We want you to take this beautiful job. It's going to pay you all this money. It's going to make you a star.'"

A sense of disappointment comes through as these people look back on their careers. Middle age, regardless of race, is a period when people review their lives; some regret past choices, even if they are by objective standards successful. Among people who were firsts in history, expectations about making a difference and achieving economic success may run even higher than the norm, and their disappointment that much greater.

Chapter 6

Peacekeepers, Crisis Managers, and Conciliators

> I can think of at least three or four instances where [the company] would have gotten [very] stringent sanctions from the EEOC and I interceded and basically negotiated [the] sanctions down . . . one or two levels. I would get informal agreements that the company could comply with. I [also] kept them out of trouble with the minority employees, who were pushing for better participation in management, and promotions, and salary increases. And I did it without selling anybody out. When I came in, there was talk of boycotts and everything by . . . certain groups of employees. In fact they did call Reverend Jesse Jackson in a couple of times. Jesse Jackson and I . . . worked things out. Yeah, . . . I kept [the corporate] hind end out of trouble a couple of times, at least.
>
> —Urban affairs director in the consumer goods industry

✦ Black executives remained in racialized jobs because white corporate leadership needed them there. The executives reaped economic rewards and enhanced social status, while their employers received a reliable work force to "absorb" black demands and government regulations. Companies who had to adjust to new social demands looked to these executives to (1) help companies conform to federal legislation, (2) reduce pressure from the external black community, (3) maintain racial harmony inside the company, and (4) help companies increase or protect their share of the black consumer market.

Conforming to Legislation

When Title VII of the 1964 Civil Rights Act was enacted, companies stepped up efforts to comply with federal employment regulations. After 1965 major corporations sought black manpower from historically neglected sources (Freeman 1976:176). That is, white employers began to recruit from previously ignored, or little-known, black colleges. They also began researching, developing, and implementing affirmative-action programs. The EEOC reported that it had advised 6,517 private sector employers in 1974 on recognizing and correcting discriminatory employment practices. The commission noted that the startling increase in its caseload resulted from an increase in federal compliance activity and in court decisions, as described in Chapters 3 and 4 (U.S. Equal Employment Opportunity Commission 1978). As corporate accommodation to federal regulations spread, the need for a cadre of managers to help companies alter discriminatory personnel practices also grew. In personnel management, for example, blacks assisted white companies in the hands-on recruitment and training of blacks. Sixty of the seventy-six executives I interviewed reported that they were instrumental in either starting or expanding minority recruitment programs to meet federal hiring guidelines. These executives also paved the way for the entry and promotion of blacks inside white-dominated institutions to meet affirmative-action requirements and protect government contracts. Indeed, twenty-six of the fifty-one (51 percent) who filled racialized jobs during the 1960s and 1970s were instrumental in helping top management detect exclusionary hiring practices and reorient personnel departments to conform to government requirements. Moreover, twelve of the twenty-six (about 46 percent) continued to specialize in this area.

The career of the head of affirmative action for a multinational diversified retailer reflects this trend. In 1966, this executive became the first black professional woman ever hired by the company. In 1970, she became the company's first black in personnel at any level, including file clerk and typist. At the time she was hired, the firm — a huge supplier of commercial goods to the U.S. Department of Defense and therefore accountable to compliance regulations — had in place an explicit set of procedures for excluding black applicants from all but the most menial of jobs. This woman started in sales in Gary, Indiana, but her status as the only black woman professional in the company gained her the attention of top management. After a series of interviews with the company's CEO, she was handpicked by him to go to Chicago and "clean up" personnel practices.

> The CEO made it a point to know me personally once I came to the company. I would say, being the first black woman [professional], he watched how I handled myself for a long time. Once he saw I was competent, and got along with [white] people, and didn't cause a lot of trouble, we had a series of talks. He told me he wanted me to be his ambassador in personnel. We discussed that possibility for a long time. He didn't want me to do anything rash, but he wanted [me to be his] eyes and ears in that department.

Under the company's double standards for pay and benefits based on race, blacks received less compensation and fewer or no job benefits. Moreover, the company used a code to channel black applicants into "suitable" jobs, such as janitorial work, and to designate which of two sets of skills tests would be used to evaluate job applicants. After the executive reported these procedures to the CEO, most of the most blatant were discontinued. She then designed and implemented the company's first affirmative-action program, including goals and timetables.

By reducing her firm's vulnerability to contract compliance reviews, this woman helped protect millions of dollars in contract awards. "There was no way the company was going to take a chance on losing those [federal] contracts," she said. "Even if we had contracts held up for two days, and it's worth millions, you are losing thousands of dollars [a day]." Ultimately, she was promoted to company director of affirmative action for helping the company avoid the costs and disruptions accompanying governmental sanctions.

This executive was important to the company not only for helping it conform to federal requirements, but also for her ability to act on behalf of top management. While not attempting to radically restructure the system, she managed to "keep them out of trouble."

Being a trusted company person carries with it costs as well as benefits. A recurring theme in the interviews was that affirmative-action jobs were easy to get into, but often hard to get out of, particularly if the executives had earned the company's trust. That dynamic was at work in the career of a forty-three-year-old group director of human resources interviewed in 1986. Starting out in the private sector in mainstream personnel, he moved quickly into an affirmative-action job, although the field was never his career goal. His reasons for moving into the racialized job path resembled those of others: He felt the pull of his black identity and an attendant obligation to help the black community. His ambition, whetted by corporate perquisites and financial rewards that come with performing a valued job, also played a role in his decision. But what began as a mutually beneficial duet became a tug of war when he tried to get out of his racialized position. Ultimately, he failed. His ability to read what the company wanted to accomplish and his success in creating an effective program conspired against him. In other words, this human resource director was a loyal company man and a highly competent black professional, qualities that made him more valuable in affirmative action than in the mainstream of the company. Finally, his salaried job offers in the private sector became defined by that function.

Tracing this executive's career in detail provides an object lesson in the dangers of doing a racialized job too well. He started in 1966 working in one of the old poverty programs, the Opportunity Industrialization Center, a skills-training center for the hard-core unemployed. He then moved into the private sector as a (mainstream) employment manager for a nationally known bakery, where he stayed for the next three years. In 1970, a white headhunter approached him about a personnel job in his current employer's Illinois plant. The opening was in a large, rapidly growing department that seemed to offer greater chances for advancement than the bakery, and he became optimistic about getting the job when the headhunter told him he was "exactly what the company was looking for." During his job interview, the personnel director said that the company needed "more black managers" and that "the opportunities are really there if you have any skills and ability." The company was, and still is, a big government contractor, and this man was the first black in the company's history to become part of plant management.

Between 1970 and 1972, the Illinois complex grew from 450 to 2,200 employees and expanded from one to three plants. When the dust settled, a general personnel manager was at the top of the personnel hierarchy, and reporting to him were three plant personnel managers and a newly created employment and training manager. Until this point, this man had been happy as a plant personnel manager and, given a choice, would have stayed in that job. Instead, the company brought in three outside people to staff the human resources program and slotted him as the employment and training manager — a move that may have been connected to the racialized functions associated with that newly created position. The Office of Federal Contract Compliance Programs (OFCCP) was most active in that period, and this man reported that he was heavily involved with increasing the proportion of employees who were minorities. "The employment function controlled the affirmative-action program for the location," he said. "That was my job. I had to ensure that we had black applicants to go into the jobs that we filled. And to be sure we filled them in a ratio that was at least in compliance with federal regulations. As far as the programming of it was concerned, it was my responsibility."

The complex was the company's largest and highest-profile facility. Between that visibility and the acknowledged difficulty of maintaining compliance in a rapidly increasing work force, the manager's results in employee relations and affirmative-action successes won him positive attention from company leadership. One year later, the company created a national affirmative-action operation and offered this manager the job. He attributed the offer to his demonstrated success and the company's need for a nationally coordinated program. I suspect that the company also saw that having a black representative run this office not only signaled the company's good intent but, given the tenor of the times, was a political necessity.

After noting that in the early 1970s most affirmative-action managers were black, he said, "I had become the [company's] highest-ranking black personnel person in the country. I guess from that standpoint they looked at me as a likely suspect. I guess I shouldn't say suspect. They came and said, 'We've got this new slot. We'd like you to come to Chicago and talk to us about it.' In a series of three interviews I was offered the job, and I took it." He had reservations about accepting the job, for he believed that "sometimes the company wants to pigeonhole you," and his objective "was not to be in affirmative action for the rest of my life."

He recognized the job's attractions, however. For instance, he believed that taking the job was "probably the fastest way to hop slots." Also, he felt an obligation to "give back" to other blacks and help the black community. After hearing what the job was designed to do, he said, "I [didn't] know if I trusted anybody else to have the commitment to the job that I thought I would have." Thus, at the time, the offer appeared to be a golden opportunity: a chance to advance his career and to play a significant role increasing opportunities for others in the black community. Nevertheless, before accepting the job he exacted the promise that he would remain in it no longer than three years, and he asked, he said, "about other jobs I could go to from here. This was [not] to be a forever job."

The company was true to its promise. In 1976, he was transferred from affirmative action into a mainstream position as a personnel manager at the company's headquarters. But even with an affirmative-action program in place, in about 1978 "[the company] still didn't have any black vice-presidents and black account managers, and black marketing managers, or female, or Hispanic, or anything else." He said that "top management was very aware that PUSH [(Jesse Jackson's People United to Save Humanity) was] out there . . . doing covenants" with big companies. Specifically, "much of PUSH's involvement was brought about by black employees' discontent . . . black people inside [these companies] . . . were disgruntled and complaining [that] somebody's got to do something about [white] people."

Since the company was based in Chicago, which is also the headquarters for Jackson's organization, it was no surprise to this man when the senior vice-president of human resources approached him with an offer. The request, if indeed the senior vice-president was merely asking, was for him to develop an internal compliance program and do what was necessary for the company to avoid bad public relations and maintain black consumer alliances.

> My perspective was I wanted to contribute, but you can't continue planning all your life, for affirmative action anyway. I've since learned that you can. I actually turned the job down when it was first offered. And [the senior vice president of human resources] came back again and said, "You know, we could go outside and we could probably bring somebody in, but . . . we would have lost some opportunities for effectiveness. We'd be in a position . . . to give you assurance that you're not going to be stuck in the job if you will accept that responsibility."

In that position, his value to the company would be based not solely on his ability to do the job but also in the fact that he was both black and a known and dependable commodity in the company. Indeed, the company's repeated attempts to coax him into the jobs suggests that top management was highly comfortable with him. His unique value to the company was further underscored by top management's offer of a significant salary increase, which he described as "worthy of making the move."

A corporate manager might turn down his superiors' request once and still be seen as a team player. But to remain competitive in most corporate environments, one would certainly not decline twice. He took the job because he believed he could eventually leave it with the blessings of his superior and, conversely, because he could not turn it down without endangering his career.

Two years after accepting the job, after, he said, "an internal analysis, and after we avoided the charges, and the compliance reviews, and the threats of being brought into litigation," the company rewarded his performance by mainstreaming him. In a move that signaled the company's commitment to his ultimate career development in human resource management, he became a manager of compensation. The company continued to groom him by further expanding his experience and, one year later, moving him laterally to regional personnel manager.

Regional personnel manager was typically a feeder job into the group director job, yet his career took another detour in 1983 into an urban affairs/EEO position.

> We talked about the fact that I'd paid my dues on the job, and that there is only so much that you can do before you begin to repeat yourself, and a number of other things. They went off and came back a second time and said, "How can we make this job appealing enough for you to reconsider?" I asked for quite a bit — and I [told them] I'm not a career affirmative-action person. And unless I can look forward to [being] one of the group's personnel heads, then I'm not interested in that job.

He remained as urban affairs director for almost three years before the company made the director of human resources job available in 1985.

A reasonable interpretation of this man's career in 1986 was that he had paid his dues in affirmative action and received his payoff, an upper level midmanagement mainstream job. However, the company was sold to a new parent company in the late 1980s, and the new leadership's assessment of him greatly differed from that of his former superiors, he said. Under the former management, he repeatedly was slotted into affirmative-action jobs because he was trusted by senior management and considered a loyal team player. But the new senior managers looked at his record and viewed him as an affirmative-action manager, a regulatory person, and someone who might prove adversarial.

Even outside that company, potential employers defined his skills by his detours, even though he did not present himself as a career affirmative-action person. By 1992, he had left the corporate world, feeling forced out, and started his own business. One reading of this career trajectory is that reentering the mainstream after performing racialized assignments may depend on a series of fortunate circumstances that happen to befall an executive.

Reducing Pressure from External Black Groups

After the mid-1960s, corporations found strategies other than affirmative-action programs to adjust to the political climate. Community relations, job training, and other urban affairs programs, essentially appeasement functions that provided service and technical assistance to black ghettos, were now deemed urgent because of the fear of racial violence.

Between 1965 and 1970, at least eighty-two Fortune 500 companies started some kind of black economic development and employment program to "principally help discourage boycotts, violence, and other threats to company well-being." In 1970, 201 of 247 city-based Fortune 500 companies reported having urban affairs programs, but only four such programs existed before 1965 (Cohn 1975). Thus, at least 197 of the 500 largest companies in the United States started urban affairs programs within the five-year period characterized by civil disorder, which included the most costly outbreaks of urban riots in the country's history.

Initially, white managers filled urban affairs jobs (Cohn 1975). But increasing the presence of African Americans allowed corporations to initiate programs to appease black communities without siphoning off white employees from other areas of the company. Moreover, the political activism of both middle- and lower-class blacks, including the grass-roots demand for black representation, necessitated naming blacks to represent the company and direct these programs. Seventeen of the fifty-one executives in this study who held racialized jobs during the 1960s and 1970s functioned to reduce pressure from black groups that were external to the company. Eleven of these seventeen (65 percent) stayed in them for most of their career.

Within the context of the times, workers filling external relations jobs were useful for easing tensions between the white corporate world and black America. In one case, an executive I interviewed moved into a community relations function in 1967 when, he said, the city was "undergoing a little upheaval, a little racial unrest, maybe, for want of a better term." Community groups were staging sit-ins that escalated to near riots in the East Coast town where company headquarters were located. This executive was approached by his mentor because "there was nobody [black] there," referring to the corporate offices. (This situation is reminiscent of the frustrated manager in Chapter 5 who was employed to coordinate the manpower-training program for a steel company after management began to perceive urban riot as a threat to the company's assets. In both cases, company headquarters — and thus huge capital investments — were located in riot-torn neighborhoods.)

Another case further explicates executives' value in buttressing vulnerable companies in urban areas. An executive who filled the urban affairs position for a midwestern bank in the late 1960s, after one of the "long hot summers" of race riots, established tutorial and summer employment programs, although banking is not a seasonal employer. His goal, he said, was to show "responsiveness on the part of the institution," thereby decreasing the bank's vulnerability in the case of future riots. To emphasize this point, he explained somewhat sardonically that the bank created the urban affairs function after "the natives jumped out and started to burn down the city. The bank saw what riots could do, and they had assets to protect." Unlike businesses that retreated to the relative peace of white suburbia, banks could not reasonably move their headquarters out of the city, he explained. For example, proximity of the bank to the Federal Reserve enabled the institution to keep money longer, since the time it took to transfer money was minimal. Bank officials weighed the cost of potential riot-related property damage against the benefits of an inner-city location. Their solution: to create an urban affairs department, viewed "by top management as an investment in the city and . . . in its own security," he said.

He described his job in the late 1960s and early 1970s as a "consultant to the top house," meaning he met directly with the top managers, he said, "to change the way the bank did business with blacks." Both he and the bank's management team believed that he could "keep them out of trouble" since he held membership in the group by which the bank felt threatened. His success in developing the bank's relationship with the black community was well rewarded. In the early 1970s, the bank's board of directors voted to make him a vice-president and director, and thus the highest-ranking African American executive in one of the country's largest banks.

In a similar situation, a black executive for a steel company was promoted to project manager in 1974, after a major construction contract worth millions of dollars came under attack by the *Chicago Defender,* an African American newspaper. Both the African American media and community that surrounded the construction site publicly criticized the company, pointing to its complete lack of African American suppliers and contractors. As this manager summarized it, "I was one of the few blacks [in the company] and I was pointed out. [The company wanted me to get] them out of trouble . . . because they were in big trouble. [Blacks] were threatening to picket the bank [that provided the loan for the project] . . . and [the company] was in trouble [because of] the minority community which was threatening the project." This man could easily maneuver between the corporate and black communities. Born and raised in a segregated black community, he had also earned a bachelor's degree from Dartmouth, an elite white college, and wanted to succeed in the white world.

Other executives among those I interviewed who held external relations jobs described their roles as corporate ambassadorships. They plugged corporations into black civil rights and social service organizations and, in general, represented white companies in black-dominated settings whenever necessary. A director of urban affairs, for example, said that in 1971, one of the reasons they hired me [as their director of community affairs] was because I knew everybody in town. I came up working with all the grass-roots organizations from all the neighborhoods. [The role was to] make [the company] look good. I did what they needed done to look good in the community. They utilized me in that fashion. For eleven years I was just their spook who sat by the door, and I understood that. Certainly I was, and I charged them well for it.

Each of the executives in this category was skilled at brokering the interests of their companies and successfully "absorbing" the tensions between white companies and urban black constituencies. The manager recruited by his mentor was able to appease protesters and reinstate order in the company headquarters town by developing a series of black-oriented outreach programs and becoming visible to the black community. The steel manager's impact on the community went further; since the corporation was involved in rebuilding the area after the riots, he also was able to improve job training and employment chances for blacks, at least temporarily. Finally, the man at the midwestern bank developed vehicles to "promote the bank's visibility and good name" and thereby created a reservoir of goodwill in the black community.

Racialized jobs were a sort of black ambassadorship, with black executives negotiating with African American activists to avoid pressure and bad publicity that threatened corporate operations and profits. Color and culture were integral to jobs to "cool out" and "keep a lid on" blacks and to manage other sources of political pressure. When blacks demanded race-based reparations during the 1960s and early 1970s, they also demanded "maximum feasible participation." This included having black representatives at all levels of an organization to convey a black perspective. As one executive I interviewed put it, "Blacks would be surrounding a company saying, 'We don't want to talk to some flunky or some white guy, we want to talk to a black vice-president.' "

Furthermore, according to one business and civic leader in Chicago, high-profile operations such as mortgage pools, private initiative councils (PICs), and other federally funded, privately run skills-training programs were started after the riots "to create economic incentives and create a feeling that things will get better for people that have been left out of prosperity."[1] The executives who administered these programs played key roles in eliciting feelings of social investment among black people.

In contrast to mainstream external relations in which corporate concern over blacks' goodwill and well-being was all but absent, racialized versions of these jobs were links to previously neglected populations, forged to appease blacks and discourage racial violence (Cohn 1975).

Maintaining Racial Harmony inside Companies

Racialized roles also neutralized race-related pressures inside corporations, where black executives mediated antagonistic, and potentially explosive, black-white relationships. Thirty of the fifty-one racialized managers I interviewed described racially volatile labor relations between black workers and white management. As in the case of external pressures, in internal conflicts they interceded as interpreters and conciliators, explaining black political action, interceding in racial conflicts, and, in general, ameliorating the racial tensions that played out inside the work environment.

They were able, for example, to bridge the widening gap between black labor's discontent and the apprehensions and bewilderment of top management. One executive was asked by the CEO of a major oil company to become management's agent in a racially sensitive work situation, explaining and then quieting blacks' organized resistance to company policy. In 1968 the company had a flourishing ghetto of lower-paid jobs occupied by African Americans who were becoming increasingly vocal in their grievances. Complaints stemmed from their systematic segregation and concentration into a single department at company headquarters and into selected low-paying occupations. Black workers who had, in general, been docile about their job stagnation became militant. When, both individually and collectively, they stationed themselves outside executive offices to demand racial justice in job competition, this man—the only black supervisor employed in the building—was selected by top management to address the situation.

> I was called [from the accounts department] into the president's office, and two senior vice-presidents were there. They didn't understand what was going on in [the] department, and they called me in to explain it. Now I wasn't the organizer of this thing. But I guess because I was the senior black in that department they asked me. That was the first meeting. The second meeting they called me in, not to explain it, but to stop it. And I guess I've been the company's affirmative-action person from that day on.

The need to contain the potentially damaging effects of the workers' political activities on the company's day-to-day operations broadened the value of this worker in the eyes of top management. Once he shifted out of account services, he became a well-paid expert, advising senior executives on the new etiquette of race relations. Given the degree of black activism at the time, he was more valuable to the company as a "cultural consultant" than in his former supervisory role. While his job as intermediary was not one that he had envisioned for himself, it would have been to his disadvantage to decline the assignment. Tensions in the company were running high. "I was in a position where somebody upstairs asked me to take this on. I couldn't turn down the top man's request without a very good reason," he said. Revealing the uniqueness of his status, and his value in the eyes of top management, he said, "They wanted me, [and] I told them what it would take to get me. I was at the top of my game where I was, so they were going to have to pay."

As in the case of the human resources director mentioned earlier, this worker was valued not solely for his color but also because top management was comfortable having him act on its behalf. Why else would he have, as he put it, "got what I wanted"? He said, "I got more money with nobody reporting to me than I got with ten people reporting to me, [a] $25,000 [pay] increase." He could not have gotten this raise solely on the basis of race, although the company felt it needed a black person badly in this role. An unknown quantity would be too risky a gamble in this volatile environment. The company wanted someone trustworthy, and just any black person would not do.

Given the scrutiny of top management and the level of racial animosity that existed in the company, one wonders how this manager would have fared in the company had he failed. He didn't fail and ended up, as he put it, "staying in affirmative-action forever, [because] they do what it takes to keep you satisfied."

Another manager's case is strikingly similar. A black director of testing in a mainstream technical job, he was deployed into personnel management to work at reducing racial tensions inside the company. As in the corporation cited earlier, job opportunities for black workers in this company were restricted to clerical activities. One-third of employees were black, and most were "secretaries and [office] administrative types." Ghettoized into a low-paying job sector, black employees developed highly disruptive strategies in protest. As in the previous case, senior management told the executive "that there was a lot of dissatisfaction in the ranks, [and] there was a definite need for someone [black] to be visible in personnel." The issue, of course, was not that "someone" be visible, since a white personnel manager was already in place. Rather, it was that the "someone" be black. He acknowledged this when he said his job was to "make blacks in the company feel they were being related to, . . . to present a positive image to the staff, [and] to show them they could make it." In short, this African American manager could offer what his white counterpart could not, a presence both politically meaningful and pacifying to blacks.

Protecting Product Markets

Given the volatility that prevailed among blacks in the 1960s and 1970s, retail companies in a competitive marketplace exploited and protected their existing market shares by hiring black salespeople to court and keep black consumers. Ten of the fifty-one executives in racialized jobs were hired or promoted specifically into sales slots oriented toward a black consumer constituency. For example, a vice-president who began his career as a sales agent for an insurance company recalled that he was hired in 1971 because his employer "saw that the black market in Rockford [Illinois] was . . . untapped." Consequently, the company "was really looking for someone to take [on sales] in the black community." This man lacked previous sales experience, and sales was not a career path he had planned to take. However, the company developed a race-specific need, so he took advantage of the opportunity.

Another executive, who worked for a major retail company in Washington, D.C., noted that he and twelve other blacks were hired by the company at about the same time, and that all were placed in stores in the inner city.

Historically, consumption patterns generally have not been considered race related. But beginning in the mid-1960s, black advertising agencies convinced companies that blacks related to distinctive cultural symbols, and market research firms showed that black consumers had unique buying patterns. Using blacks in sales was one way to project an image that would attract black consumers. Moreover, although political pressures have since lessened, consumer goods companies still use race to enhance their image among black consumers. For example, McDonalds has a series of television advertisements that was created by a black-owned advertising firm, features black rap artists, and is directed to black audiences.

Using blacks in sales is primarily a response to markets, but during the 1960s and 1970s, black executives also assumed racialized roles as intermediaries between white corporations and black buyers in response to race-based political pressures. Companies during that period were threatened with boycotts that could have withdrawn large segments of buyers from their existing consumer base. The rise of one executive employed by an educational testing and supplies company is an example of how corporations responded to such pressures. In an era when blacks were demanding more representation and community control, a change in a New Orleans school district's management put blacks in key buying positions. This man was promoted, in 1965, from an entry level customer representative to manager of community relations, after his company was threatened with losing a lucrative market in the school district. He stated flatly that he was promoted because "the company was abruptly shut out, [and] they needed somebody black to represent [them]" to this new sales constituency. In other words, he was assigned to a highly visible sales position because a black presence in that role would project a message of corporate responsiveness to black concerns and racial sensitivity. Black buyers for the school district could then feel good about patronizing the company.

For similar reasons, several managers were assigned to administer politically inspired, but economically motivated, business programs. For instance, after black consumers joined ranks with civil rights advocates to boycott products, set-aside programs were established by companies to allocate a percentage of their purchases to minority businesses. One executive oriented a major retailer's urban affairs program to black business development after the company was threatened with boycotts.

Relative to his white peers in the company, this man had moved rapidly up the mainstream corporate ladder. A counter clerk in 1964, within three years he had moved through a series of supervisory slots to become a store manager. At the age of twenty-three, he was making $23,000 a year: a $10,000 salary and a $13,000 performance-based bonus.[2] "Running the stores was a piece of cake. I was dazzled by the money and very self-confident," he said. Company officials soon began considering him for middle management. An advisor told him to apply for a promotion because he had both the talent and the skills to take on more responsibility. In 1967, he moved from store management to area supervisor. Coming up through the ranks was the typical route for the company's top executives and, therefore, "the way to go," he said.

Less than a year after his promotion, however, he was asked to apply for a job creating an urban affairs program for the company. The circumstances that led to this request were relatively straightforward. The company viewed blacks as a sizable proportion of its customer base, and civil rights activists had confronted the company with specific demands backed by the threat of a nationwide boycott. The selection process differed significantly from that used to fill other jobs at the same level. It included interviews with the head of personnel, a senior vice-president, the head of licensing, the corporate legal council, and the president of the company, "real heavy hitters," as he said. He was offered, and accepted, the job, which was "to work with the licensee department and [come] up with minority candidates around the country to become [store owners]."

Within this operations-driven corporation, a manager with demonstrated talent for business operations, particularly one who had a senior management mentor, would generally be considered a serious contender for a top level mainstream position. Slotting such an employee into urban affairs might appear to be a frivolous use of talent. But in 1968, with no other blacks working at the company's corporate offices (save for one janitor), the company was vulnerable to racial protest. From this perspective, deploying a black midlevel manager, a known commodity in the company, into corporate urban affairs was a rational business decision.

In their book on black executives, Davis and Watson (1982) report that the first blacks hired into management during the 1960s believed they were valued by companies as much for color and image as for any other characteristics. In the case of this midlevel manager, using a black to negotiate with black activists could defuse charges of racism that community leaders had leveled at the company. It also cast a member of the activists' constituency as a representative of the company, thus creating a symbol of progressive interests, while minimizing differences. In this manager's case, as in others', race was at least as highly valued as any other qualification, including skill in performing a midmanagement mainstream function, and was the basis for his assignment to black business development and community relations.

While this manager's job seems straightforward — avert a boycott by creating more opportunities for blacks to be business owners — it was actually fraught with political pitfalls. He had to perform under the scrutiny of both black and company (white) constituencies with strong, and conflicting, class and race interests. He had to broker the interests of white top management, white store licensees, black candidates for store licenses, and black civil rights activists and appease whites in the company who resented what they thought of as blacks' special treatment. He was responsible for the conflicting tasks of building relationships with inner-city black groups and implementing a business program that could project a socially conscious corporate image, while also reassuring white licensees who did not want blacks in their market and who were not at all convinced that the company was moving in a good direction. Moreover, he bore the brunt of criticism from rank-and-file white employees who resented blacks' getting what they felt were "special favors." Finally, top management withheld full-fledged support because of what they perceived to be a lowering of program standards to bring more black licensees into the system.

In addition to these paradoxes, the job had a second, and inherently race-linked, set of difficulties. The company had financial criteria for franchising stores that whites could meet relatively easily but that most black licensing candidates could not. Furthermore, white banks would not lend money to black business, even though the company had a successful track record in starting up fledgling stores. Finally, blacks who had money to invest could not afford to quit their jobs and were often rejected by the company because policy stipulated the owner must also be the day-to-day operator on the premises. The executive said, "People that were declined would go to various groups, such as the NAACP, and say, 'Listen, they turned me down.'" Each of these quandaries, naturally, created its own tensions.

This manager, therefore, was saddled with what he called "an impossible task." And each of these race-linked conflicts made his career more vulnerable. In this job, the stakes were high, as was the likelihood of failure. The additional, if unintended, benefit of having a black fill such a job was the creation of a scapegoat. If the company effort failed, the black executive would take the blame from both top management and black community groups.

Affirmative-action, urban affairs, and community relations functions in companies worked in dual ways. They were mechanisms that made social and economic resources more available to the aggregate black population. They also were a system of occupations that helped to minimize change and maintain the status quo, for they alleviated political pressures on companies by defending them and deflecting attacks made on racial grounds. As a corporate tool, black executives' value was commensurate with their skill in abating political pressures, protecting profits, and not rocking the boat — not in consolidating black power and changing the makeup of an institution's power brokers.

It is easy to view these functionaries as gatekeepers and stumbling blocks to institutionalizing equality. Yet what were the alternatives? Did they, for example, hinder change more than white managers would have in similar positions? There is scant reason to believe that employers would have taken more progressive steps for blacks if these executives had not filled such roles.

Chapter 7

Blacks on the Bubble

The company was . . . eliminating a lot of positions, you know, not just mine, and [I was told the company] would not be someplace that I wanted to be. To say that I was surprised is an understatement. I guess I just didn't think I would be affected because, number one, I was the only black senior manager in the company. And I had high visibility. [I] built all kinds of goodwill for the company . . . to the point that my name was almost associated with the corporation name when I would come to a place. So, you know, I overestimated my value to the company, I guess you could say that.

—Director of community relations for a consumer goods company

✦ In the 1980s, the federal government's twenty-year commitment to policies and practices that helped blacks compete economically underwent a dramatic reversal. Throughout the decade the White House opposed race-based policies and protections, particularly the policy of affirmative action (Hudson and Broadnax 1982), and Supreme Court appointments and decisions signaled a retreat from race-based remedies to overcome historic discrimination (Wilson et al. 1991).[1]

The social and political mood of the decade was foreshadowed in the 1978 legal challenge to affirmative action by Allan Bakke, a white male who brought suit against the University of California Regents, claiming that affirmative action is "reverse discrimination" against better qualified white men and alleging that he had been discriminated against when he was denied admission to the university's medical program (Dreyfuss and Lawrence 1979; Sitkoff 1981).

The Supreme Court, in the Bakke decision, rejected the use of racial quotas to overcome the cumulative effects of past discrimination and found the special-admissions program for racial minorities unconstitutional. Although the Court subsequently ruled that race could be taken narrowly into account to remedy proven discrimination, the Bakke decision served as a prelude to the political viewpoints that would shape the 1980s. The Reagan administration took a stronger position, opposing "court-ordered and court-sanctioned racial preferences for non-victims of discrimination" (Hudson and Broadnax 1982) and actively arguing against the use of preferential treatment and quotas in employment practices (Reynolds 1983). Although the Court did twice endorse affirmative-action policies during the 1980s, most of its decisions clearly indicated that the use of preferential hiring policies was on soft ground.[2]

The attack on race-specific programs sent a strong signal that the role of the federal government as a strong advocate of African American employment was being reduced. Within this social and legal context, the question arises of whether substantive characteristics of African Americans' jobs make them particular targets to be downsized or cut from companies. I believe that the race-specific focus of these jobs makes them vulnerable to changes in the administrative structures of white corporations, which themselves fluctuate with political conditions.

Status of Jobs

In 1986, I asked the managers I interviewed if their jobs had changed in title, scope of responsibilities, budget, or functions since 1980. For example, had any of their responsibilities been increased, reassigned to other managers, or dissolved? Had departmental budgets and staff increased or decreased?

Racialized jobs in corporations were the most recent employment for about two-fifths (thirty of the seventy-six) of the managers I interviewed. Table 3 compares the reports of forty-five mainstream managers with these thirty managers in racialized jobs. (One chief

Table 3
Reports of Job Changes by Job Type

Job Changes	Racialized Jobs ($N=30$)	Mainstream Jobs ($N=45$)
Duties Downsized/Cut	50%	11%
Duties Increased/Unchanged	50%	89%

executive officer was excluded from this summary since a CEO might be fired by a corporate board but the job itself would not be increased, downsized, or eliminated.) The table conforms to what my hypothesis would predict. African American executives in racialized jobs, much more than African American executives in mainstream jobs (50 percent versus 11 percent), reported that the company had eliminated, reduced, or redistributed their functions to managers in other areas. The relevance of these reports may be seen as dependent upon comparing them to those of white managers, but my analysis links fragility to the characteristics of jobs rather than to the characteristics of job holders. Thus, I compare structures of occupations while keeping race constant. Hypothetically, whites concentrated in racialized jobs would confront the same economic fate. Comparing the status of managers by race, per se, is less pertinent to my argument than illustrating a specific type of occupational fragility.

The vulnerability associated with racialized jobs is evident in the career of a vice-president of urban affairs who started out in the financial industry in the early 1970s in affirmative action. The intensity of racial pressures in Chicago caused his job to evolve into a community liaison position that focused on placating blacks. He summarizes his job this way: "I kept my hands on the pulse of the [black] community — I sold the bank's story out to the community. I conducted the social audit, finding out where the bank was deficient, where they could come up to speed." This manager makes explicit the difference between the futures of the two tracks in public relations, mainstream and racialized (i.e., related to the problems of African Americans). The mainstream functions are responsible for maintaining traditional (white) civic contributions. The racialized function for which this manager was responsible was essentially an appeasement role. By the late 1970s, the rationale for appeasement no longer existed in Chicago; pressure from blacks was absent. The community affairs function oriented to African Americans was cut back, as the manager explained.

> They kept talking, they had this term, "the long hot summer," and up to about 1976 [or] 1977, they were talking about the long hot summer [but] nothing happened. [So] they just cut the money. I mean, their traditional lines of support . . . for the [Chicago] symphony, and the [Chicago] Art Institute and those kinds of things, they were still maintaining a level. But no [money for] community groups, grass-roots types. There was just a withdrawal.

African American executives in mainstream as well as in racialized jobs reported reductions in responsibility that suggest career vulnerability (see Table 3). Such vulnerability in the climate of the 1980s, then, cannot be viewed merely as a product of racial inequality in the job structure. The job fragility of white-collar workers, including middle managers and financial industry employees, is a feature of macroeconomic changes such as greatly diminished growth in service sector jobs (Hertz 1990; Starobin 1993).[3]

An example among the executives I interviewed is a vice-president of sales for a publishing company who indicated that his company changed dramatically when the breakup of phone companies made the business climate in the mid-1980s "far more competitive and risky than ever before." I asked if he felt his job might be threatened as a result of increased competition, which is a market-mediated source of job fragility. He responded, "Well, yes, if our new competitors get a disproportionate share of the work that we used to get. No, if all those contracts come back to us." Indeed, in the late eighties era of corporate mergers and economic restructuring, both white and African American managers were victims of job loss in major corporations, according to a 4 January 1987 *New York Times* article, "The Ax Falls on Equal Opportunity," and a 1987 piece in

U.S. News and World Report, "You're Fired." Job insecurity confronts all individuals in high-status occupations, not blacks per se. We can still ask, however, whether there are substantive differences within this strata of jobs that make the fragile position of African Americans in management a somewhat different phenomenon.

The experiences of the executives I interviewed illustrate how politically useful jobs in white companies can become economically expendable, particularly in a context of corporate buyouts and economic reorganization. A director of community affairs and public affairs who managed the African American component of public relations for a major retail firm in Chicago had since 1972 been charged with "keeping [up] the image" of the company in the African American community and representing the company at conventions, on community boards, and on the committees of African American community organizations. Between 1981 and 1982 the company began streamlining the work force to maximize profits; similar to the case just recounted, when pressure waned, the company image among African American consumers became less important. During this period, the director reported, his job in community affairs "just wasn't important to them — they just didn't want to spend money on that any more." He said that "they wanted to cut the job, they just didn't want to cut me" when the component of community affairs oriented to African Americans was dismantled completely. Unable to shift successfully into a new role, he took an early retirement.

A second individual, also in community affairs, observed that his employer had become "a very different company" than the one he entered. He went on to say that "there were certainly some things I had to unlearn," because "everything [became] tied to [profit]. And [my job] could not be tied to . . . revenue, at least in an immediate sense. For over fifteen years I needed to be tuned in to what blacks in the grass-roots community were thinking. But Chicago is changing. Now, all of a sudden, I [was not] getting any of the support I needed."

Other managers in racialized jobs told similar stories. For instance, a twenty-year manager of corporate contributions and community relations for a steel company told me he was "looking for opportunities elsewhere." He reported that the programs he ran were funded by company reserves set aside during the 1960s and 1970s following rioting by African Americans in Chicago. These once large reserves diminished as company profits fell in the 1980s. In that comparatively calm racial atmosphere the incentive to tap limited reserves cooled. He said that his department "will have a totally different look. . . . [It] will honor the commitments we made for this year and phase out. That includes me and part of my staff."

Even managers who have not experienced immediate reductions say that racialized functions are easy targets because the political climate changed at the same time that corporations reorganized. Among them is a manager who had designed a minority purchasing program for his company and was considering retirement. The company began streamlining in 1984, reducing purchasing requirements and its base of minority and majority suppliers.

> They haven't tried to cut back my program; my budget grows every year. But they're trying to eliminate the supplier base. . . . They reduced it by half between last year and this, and they want to reduce it again by half next year. [Question: Do you think the company will fill your job once you leave?] No. When I leave I'm not even grooming anybody to take my job. As far as I know I don't think the company is [grooming anyone] either.

The highly specialized, once flourishing job was created to assist African Americans and other minority businesspeople during the 1970s gain company contracts through a minority set-aside program, typical of those developed by companies in response to mass demonstrations and consumer boycotts by African Americans. The program's mainstream, less specialized counterpart in the area of purchasing, although vulnerable in the 1980s, remained in place in the 1990s. But by the early 1990s the manager's part of the purchasing function, oriented toward African Americans, was dismantled and allowed to dissolve. Interviews support the conclusion that racialized jobs were created when economic expansion and race-specific employment demands converged. In the 1980s these trends reversed. Political pressure placed on employers by government and the African American public weakened. At the same time, competition for market share intensified. Racialized functions, therefore, have greatly reduced value.

The restrained federal approach to racial issues and the relative political quiescence of African Americans, in conjunction with economic transitions, undermined these jobs and made them rational targets for companies to let go. It is the intersection of deracialization and instability in the economy that creates a different (i.e., race-based) fragility to these managers' positions.

Job Security

I have predicted that the stability of racialized jobs would vary according to conditions, which suggests that a race-based structure of job opportunities actually works both ways. Where pressure declines, jobs become unstable; but where pressure is stable, so are these jobs. Race would make African Americans in these jobs vulnerable, but these jobs can also protect African Americans from job loss. This notion of a two-way street is supported by those managers with racialized responsibilities who did not express concern about their future in a company. These were that half of the managers (fifteen of thirty) who reported that their jobs had not been downgraded or cut (refer to Table 3). Yet these managers do not undermine my thesis that fragility is a component in racialized careers. Five executives identified current sources of political pressure on their employers.

Table 4 summarizes job changes among the thirty executives working in race relations. The jobs are sorted into two fields: affirmative action and community relations. I classified managers with EEO, personnel, and staff-training functions as mostly engaged in affirmative action, and managers with urban affairs, corporate contributions, marketing, and public relations functions as doing community relations work. Their experience showed that people who

Table 4
Reports of Job Changes by Racialized Job Type

Job Changes	Affirmative Action Jobs (N=13)	Community Relation Jobs (N=17)
Duties Downsized/Cut	67%	35%
Duties Increased/Unchanged	33%	65%

filled affirmative-action jobs faced fewer cuts than those filling community affairs jobs. About one-third of the managers (four of thirteen) in affirmative action reported job cuts compared to two-thirds (eleven of seventeen) in community relations.

Affirmative-action jobs stem from government requirements, a less volatile source of political pressure than community relations jobs, and they have been less vulnerable to cutbacks because the federal regulatory apparatus has not been dismantled. For instance, two affirmative-action managers who reported that their responsibilities had increased also reported that their current employer was under a consent decree. The rationale that created these jobs still remains, in spite of some attenuation in attention or enforcement. Even if a company wished to cut affirmative-action slots, it would still have government regulations and visits from compliance officers to contend with.

In contrast, African American jobs in community relations have proven more vulnerable, consistent with my notion of a politically mediated class position, for they were created in response to community pressures and company desire for visibility among African American constituencies. The greater variability in community-based political pressures compared to governmental legislation makes decline of community relations jobs more volatile.

A leading consumer goods company in Chicago illustrates these points. In 1989, the company was targeted for protest by a group of community activists because of its poor minority-hiring record. To avert a bad, and potentially embarrassing, public relations image, a mainstream company job in corporate giving was transformed into a community affairs job, and a new community affairs (African American) manager hired to negotiate with a small, but vocal, group of activists. In 1993, the company underwent corporate restructuring; in view of black community indifference at the time, the community affairs functions of this job declined. In 1994, the continued quiescence of blacks enabled the company to let the midlevel African American community relations manager go. When last I heard, he had moved to a lower-paid job in another midwestern city.

The case of Rebuild L.A. is a second illustration of how much more variable the cycles of community relations jobs are relative to affirmative-action jobs. Rebuild L.A. was created in 1992 as a clearinghouse for channeling more social and economic resources into the riot-torn areas of Los Angeles. A community activist and union organizer reported that African Americans and Hispanics were hired by that organization into highly visible roles similar to those of community affairs managers. The activist read their presence at meetings with union and community representatives as a way to deflect sensitive issues and protect the organization's credibility. In my model of class development, these professional jobs for nonwhite workers were created directly by urban turmoil; as the fear of new riots and community turmoil abates, these jobs — even, perhaps the organization — will no longer be necessary.

Overall, the pattern of job security or job vulnerability found among managers I interviewed in either affirmative action or community relations is grounded in the residuals of political pressure. Political conditions cause racialized jobs to erode, just as political conditions create these jobs and protect them. Job security is anchored to the governmental and community pressures from African Americans that remain in place today. It is reasonable to suggest that, as pressures from the government abate (as have pressures from the African American community), affirmative-action jobs will go the way of community relations jobs and become increasingly expendable in companies. Should that be the case, affirmative-action managers' reports of job stability would support the thesis of political dependency. When pressures for antibias legislation abate, these jobs would be eliminated.

My thesis also predicts that executives employed in consumer companies would report greater job security than those in capital goods companies, because consumer companies are more visible to the public, and therefore more vulnerable to direct social pressure. Moreover, they would be relatively more vulnerable to public action than capital goods companies because the public is their buyer, not other businesses. Indeed, during the 1960s and 1970s, boycotts by African Americans were an effective tool for gaining concessions from consumer companies because they directly threatened sales in inner-city markets. Manning Marable (1983:158) notes that "between 1960 and 1973, the estimated amount of goods and services purchased by African-Americans increased from $30 billion to almost $70 billion annually. By 1978 the African-American consumer market was the ninth largest in the world." Increased competition for market share during the 1980s may have given special markets greater economic significance.

I categorized respondents according to the industry of their private sector employer in 1986, coding companies such as McDonalds Corporation and Kraft as consumer/retail companies and companies such as Container Corporation of America and Brunswick as capital goods/manufacturing companies. The twenty-one managers employed in capital goods companies were more likely to report post-1980 job cuts than managers in consumer goods companies. Eight (38 percent) reported their jobs were cut or downsized, but seven of the nine managers (78 percent) employed in consumer goods reported this change. Whether this relationship holds when other factors are controlled was not part of my investigation, but it is at least consistent with what my thesis would predict. And, indeed, the potential for black consumer pressure during the 1980s remained just below the surface. PUSH orchestrated a boycott and negative publicity campaign against Nike, a sports goods manufacturer, and Anheuser-Busch to increase the representation of African Americans on their boards of directors and in managerial positions. Both companies overcame this threat to their profits. I suspect having an African American vice-president meet the press and defend the company's hiring record helped Anheuser-Busch deflect black criticism. As an African American director for public relations for a $6 billion consumer goods company in Chicago noted, "You can't be . . . based in Chicago and not fear . . . I shouldn't say fear . . . be aware of Jesse [Jackson]."

Attempts at Job Enhancement

During post-1980 cutbacks some managers tried to break out of racialized slots and into the mainstream of a company. At issue here is how much their relative success hinged on their previous work experience, and whether racialized human capital was a factor that limited their perceived value in mainstream corporate functions.

I categorized careers that incorporated some, but not a majority, of racialized jobs in 1986 as "mixed," and those composed of mostly racialized jobs in 1986 as "segregated." (I dropped executives who had held no racialized jobs from this portion of the analysis.) Although only illustrative, the following comparisons of segregated and mixed careers suggest that career segregation makes African American managers dependent on racial politics because they lack requisite experience in core corporate areas. The history of a former community relations manager for a major electronics corporation illustrates the idea that skills once in demand became a contributing factor to these managers' vulnerability. This man reported that his company's commitment to urban affairs began to decrease; observing the "handwriting on the wall," as he put it, he made multiple attempts to get out of urban affairs.

> I was just not able to make that break. I talked to [people] in various divisions that I was interested in, and I got the lip service that they would keep [me] in mind if something opened up. As it happened, that just did not develop. I can never remember being approached by anyone. Nothing [happened] . . . that I can really hang [onto] as an offer. People would ask, "Have you ever run a profit-and-loss operation?"

Finally, he describes himself as taking "hat in hand" and approaching senior management in 1982 to request duties he knew to be available in a general administrative area.

> Frankly, this was an attempt to seize an opportunity. This time I went and I asked for a [new assignment]. We had some retirement within the company and some reorganization. I saw an opportunity to help myself. The urban affairs was shrinking. A number of jobs we created [in urban affairs] were completely eliminated. It just happened that the opportunity [to pick up administrative services] was there. It had a significant dollar budget and profit-and-loss opportunity. . . . It was concrete and useful. So I asked for it.

He successfully diversified by combining urban affairs with the more stable functions of administrative services, but this strategy bought him only about two more years in the company before his job was eliminated entirely.

> You know . . . [whites] tend to stereotype black managers and say you can only do one thing. But they will take a white manager and they will allow him to try many different things, and I can think of somebody right away. But typically a black manager is pigeonholed. And he doesn't have the luxury of making a mistake either. A black manager can only make one mistake and he's branded forever.

When this man reentered the job market, the same skills that had created vulnerability in his old company were the ones for which he was in demand. Although he avoided applying for affirmative-action jobs and concentrated on administrative services, affirmative-action and related positions were the only offers that came his way.

An urban affairs manager who tried a move to warehouse distribution in a retail company was similarly constrained. He had previously constructed a successful career, but the trade-off for rising in a company in race-oriented jobs was being cut off from main-stream areas. He failed in his attempt to shift from what he termed the "money-using" to the "money-producing" part of the business. "I was too old to do what you had to do to compete. . . . I was competing with twenty-one and twenty-two year olds to get into the system. They couldn't charge [my salary] to a store and have me doing the same thing the others [were] doing [for much less money]. You need the ground-level experience. When I should have gotten it, I was busy running an affirmative-action department."

I explored with him possibilities for placement in other areas of the company. Why didn't he expand his job into mainstream public relations, an area he was apparently more qualified to pursue? He responded, "I thought about it very seriously. I wondered where I was going with the system. It came up quite often. I talked about it when I first accepted this job. And at the end. They told me, 'We don't know. We'll have to get back to you.' They never did." That his superiors never got back to him may have been because the organization needed him precisely where he was. Or it may have resulted from senior management's perception that he lacked the necessary skills to compete with younger mainstream managers who had moved up through that field.

The latter possibility is supported by the comments of a manager who was offered, and took, a job in compensation and benefits. However, he failed in his new job precisely because his past concentration in affirmative action underqualified him for it. "I moved over . . . as director," he said. "Now, mind you, I'm going from a corporate [affirmative-action] job . . . to . . . compensation and benefits. I told the chairman of the company I didn't have any experience in that field. I might not be his man."

These three men identified two routes in their attempts to buffer their position in a company, moving laterally either into an entirely different corporate area associated with mainstream planning, production, or administration or into the mainstream component of the racialized area. But the failure of their attempts show that these racialized jobs have walls; executives who specialized in affirmative action and community relations were stymied in both routes. In exchange for establishing expertise in racialized functions, these managers reduced their value in other areas.

One personnel specialist noted that moving creditable line managers into affirmative action legitimates the role in the eyes of other executives. On the other hand, he observed, individuals ought to be in such jobs only about three years, or they were lost to the larger system. And, indeed, the longer the executives studied were racialized, the greater their chances of staying racialized in a field. Because of circumscribed skills, their exclusion from in-house power networks, and their "black-only" track records, people who were concentrated in racialized roles were perceived to lack the experience to compete in mainstream company areas. The white power structure that one anointed these managers now perceives the skills that gave them value as outmoded. A director of affirmative action talked about this dead end. "Nobody ever told me . . . that if you stay in [this] job you'd be in [this] job forever. You don't move to vice-president of personnel from manager of EEO."

In sum, when economic and political challenges to corporate hiring policies abated during the 1980s, the value of racialized slots also abated. Either incumbents tried but failed to move into the corporate mainstream jobs, or they did not attempt a move because they failed to perceive another niche for themselves in their company. I asked an executive secretary of corporate contributions if, after twenty years with the company, there were other departments that could use him. He replied, "Apparently not. That's what they told me." When I asked a community affairs director if she had sought out other areas of employment in a company when her job was cut, she responded, "I didn't think there was any place in the company that I could fit."

People with mixed careers, in contrast, could enlarge their roles within core areas in the company. For example, one manager working for a major Chicago retailer had a nineteen-year career that had by 1986 alternated between personnel and labor relations and urban affairs and affirmative action. In 1985 he was appointed to replace an exiting African American vice-president of community affairs.

His new position in community affairs was a downgraded version of the old job; his title was director of community affairs. In 1986, the community affairs staff and budget once again were reduced. He explained how he aggressively enlarged his role, which had become a meaningless position.

> I . . . went into my boss and told him I could do it with one hand tied behind my back. I had a director title for something that took one day a week to do. I told him that he had to give me some more responsibilities in personnel. So that's how I got that. [The commitment to affirmative action had] gotten so bad, the firm moved its headquarters from O'Hare to Salt Lake City. I guess that's one way of getting the monkey off your back.

The fact that in the 1970s the company headquarters moved out of Chicago, with its highly politicized African American population, to a much less confrontational and predominantly white environment may indeed be part of the reason for reducing the budget for community affairs. To protect his future in the company this manager asked for, and received, more responsibilities in mainstream personnel, becoming director of community affairs and area personnel manager. Without critical experience in personnel functions, it is likely that continuing cutbacks in community affairs would have placed him in the ranks of vulnerable managers. By 1993 he had managed to shed all remnants of the racialized components of his job and acquire the title of area personnel manager.

Exiting Executives: 1986 and 1993

The theory of politically mediated opportunity structures posits that when social upheaval among African Americans abated the fragility of black professional and managerial advancement would be revealed. In 1986, eight of thirty managers in racialized jobs were leaving or had left the company with which they had been identified. None of the mainstream managers were leaving or had left.

Table 5
Characteristics of Exiting Executives

Job Title	Last Field	Exit Year	Job Status
Director	Community Relations	1982	Cut
Vice-President	Community Relations	1983	Cut
Manager	Affirmative Action	1984	Downgraded
Director	Affirmative Action	1984	Downgraded
Manager	Community Relations	1985	Cut
Vice-President	Community Relations	1986	Downgraded
Manager	Affirmative Action	1986	Downgraded

Table 5 records the status of civil rights jobs held by executives I interviewed who had left a corporation by 1986. All were either cut or downgraded. The suggestion might be made that these executives weren't talented and lacked the critical skills to compete in corporations and so were placed in racialized jobs unimportant to companies. But a review of their titles suggests that the opposite is true. Of eight exiting executives in 1986, two were functional vice-presidents. In comparison, in the same year only 4 of the 1,362 executives with a title of functional vice-president or above working in a Fortune 500 or Fortune Service 250 company (Korn/Ferry 1986) were African American. In the group of exiting managers, moreover, two were the highest-ranking African American managers in their respective companies. Another was cited in a major publication in 1982 as being among the top black managers nationwide in leading white corporations. Two managers were the first black persons to reach the level of director in their respective companies, and a third was the first to reach the level of full vice-president. One manager was among only three African American managers to succeed to the rank of midlevel manager in a company. This evidence is consistent with my point that racialized jobs were valuable functions in companies, and that in the 1980s their value unraveled.

By 1993, seven years later, thirty-six of the seventy-six people in my original study had left their companies,[4] collateral evidence that their racialized jobs — once useful for restoring peace in urban centers — are intrinsically fragile. When I compared managers in mixed and mainstream careers with those in racialized careers, I found that the latter had left their original employer at almost twice the rate of their mainstreamed counterparts (68 percent versus 35 percent). Thus, an executive's exodus depended on work experience. Theoretically, people in nonracialized careers in 1986 would fare relatively better over the decade than those in racialized careers because of the generalized nature of the functions they performed.

Executives in affirmative-action, community relations, and other black-related fields who had left companies by 1993 found that their value in the open market had eroded. Seven of the thirteen sought another position in a white corporation. The three who found jobs either moved down in job level or went to work for smaller firms in other midwestern cities. The other ten executives left the white private sector and returned to the niche that has historically supported the African American middle class — government jobs, entrepreneurship, and black self-help agencies.

As job competition intensifies, the ability of middle-class African Americans to protect and maintain their position in the broader labor market may erode. Layoff rates in managerial and professional specialty occupations almost doubled between 1981 and 1992 (Gardner 1995). One racialized executive recalled that when he was laid off in 1987, "a lot of people had not experienced it. Six years later, a hell of a lot of people have . . . — both white and black." By 1993 he had stopped worrying about his upward mobility and was looking for any stable work that would allow him to break even financially. He said, "I'm making about the same as I made in 1987, [but] I feel fortunate that I have at least landed on my feet to some extent and have a job. I've been level for all that time, but I mean, you know, what's the alternative?"

Indications are that the economic cleavage between the haves and have nots, wider than it was a decade ago, may get even wider (Starobin 1993). Under these conditions civil disorder among African Americans at the base of the economic ladder also may erupt again. At the same time, African Americans at every level feel that social justice is limited and that leaders, laws, and policies may not help them. They interpret the Los Angeles riots as an event caused by increased feelings of helplessness similar to the sense of deprivation that set off urban explosions in the 1960s. If government efforts abate and opportunities for good jobs decline, black community protest and social disruption may reach 1960s levels. Although white society is much better prepared to oppress racial uprising, the dilemma of African Americans may reemerge near the top of the national agenda. If so, roles that can explain and help calm black disruptive elements will regain prominence, and African Americans willing to fill these roles will once again be in demand.

Chapter 8

A Rash of Pessimism

> Question: When we talked in 1986, you were [more] optimistic about your future here. What changed?
>
> Answer: Moves . . . happening all around [me]. Individuals moving [up] who were at your level, who you know are not as competent and have not done as much, then you wonder. And you see others who have done a tremendous amount, either not being promoted or [being] terminated in the organization. You begin to be concerned. And I guess now I'm . . . I don't see myself as cynical, now I'm just much more realistic.
>
> —A mainstream director in a consumer goods company

✦ Racialized jobs are an obvious, but not the only, vulnerable facet of African Americans' private sector gains. In 1986, for example, a high-ranking retail executive was reputed to be "the one," a likely candidate for the first African American to head a Fortune 500 company. But his prospects for advancement in the company suddenly and dramatically altered, causing the African American business cognoscenti to radically change their assessment of him. They pointed to serious flaws in his management style. Some described him as a star in management who became too much of a company man to be a leader; others described him as too passive. Their judgment can be summarized in the words of an executive who suggested that "he gave it a good shot," but "he just didn't have it."

Beneath such sentiments lies the hope that lack of merit rather than racial discrimination produced this unsettling and unexpected career outcome. In 1986, the idea of one of their number reaching the "mahogany office" (the chief executive's office) in five or so years seemed highly possible to African American men and women in Chicago corporations. But in the 1990s, they witnessed repeated failure among African Americans as they approached positions to which they aspired. An optimistic belief in "the system" that once prevailed among nonracialized executives turned to a pessimism infused with scaled-down career expectations. In the 1980s, a forty-year-old department director boldly predicted she would one day become an officer of the company. In the 1990s the same woman, at forty-seven still a department director, planned her future in terms of "how much longer I'll be with the company, as opposed to how far up [in the company] I'll go." Executives who once buoyantly approached or occupied higher-level jobs now soberly analyze their careers and talk about their fight against downward mobility.

Face-saving explanations varied according to gender. Women tended to stress the importance of family and community over career. The forty-seven-year-old department director, for instance, pointed out that she was doing all she could to move to a higher level, "but if it doesn't work out, it doesn't matter to me anyway. I have a daughter . . . I'm active in the church . . . I'm not willing to give up my whole life to this." Men stressed the importance of their role in the company and itemized their responsibilities.

Although the self-protective stances differ, all reveal anxiety provoked by new challenges to these executives' occupational standing. A man in his midfifties offers a particularly poignant example. In 1986 he was the highest-ranking black manager in his company and the protegé of a powerful mentor. Thereafter his company downsized, his mentor left, and he held three jobs in different companies.

> You know, my life was . . . well grooved. I had everything planned to the T [and] I controlled the situation. [But] all that ended. And what happens is, you have to start all over. You . . . reorganize your lifestyle, your way of doing things, your way of thinking. All the time you . . . try to preserve some dignity. But you always go back and self-search and [ask], what did I do

wrong? What could I have done differently? Hopefully you come up with some good answers and you don't [do] too much inner destruction.

The new pessimism about career advancement among these African American executives is most apparent when the attitudes of nonracialized interviewees are compared to those reported by interviewees in racialized careers in 1986, who were about five times more likely to have had their jobs eliminated, trimmed, or dispersed. Such changes contributed both to the exit of racialized executives and to their perception that they had reached a dead end. In comparison, executives with principally mainstream experiences reported less (market-mediated) job fragility and consequently expressed much more optimism about their corporate futures. Three-quarters of mainstream compared to one-third of racialized individuals believed they had a good or excellent chance for promotion or for making a lateral move leading to promotion within five years. They also were much more likely to predict that they could replace a lost job with one at the same level or better (70 percent of mainstream executives versus 30 percent of racialized). But by the nineties, these executives on the fast track perceived changes in the organizational climate as detrimental for African Americans.

The emergence of a global economy, the continued trend in corporate downsizing, and rapid changes in workplace technology have swept aside layers of middle managers, African American and white alike (*Fortune* 1993). The old corporate norms of lifetime employment and regular promotions appear to be dissolving just when the first full generation of middle-class African Americans to benefit from civil rights–related policies arrived on the scene. In the 1990s a cohort effect has intertwined with a racial effect to short circuit black executives' careers. Most of them are now "on the beach," as one man termed it, that is, they have experienced little or no mobility since the mid-1980s. They have chosen either to hang on until they can retire, or to leave the white private sector altogether. The stars in this study are falling; the nine executives who were in the first and second executive tiers in 1986 (i.e., chief officers and senior vice-presidents) have either left their 1986 employer or simply are trying to survive in their jobs.

Informants indicate that job fluidity inside many companies has veered from historical norms. People no longer stay in their jobs over a long period of time but are moved from assignment to assignment. Nevertheless, vertical mobility that nonracialized executives once earned based on tenure and performance has become unpredictable. Since the 1986 study a sizable proportion of such individuals have stagnated inside companies; thirty-one of fifty were with the same company in 1993 that employed them in 1986.[1] Just seven of them (23 percent)—four in support positions and three in line positions—had received promotions designated by a new job title. Even individuals receiving salary increases or different sets of responsibilities since 1986 did not view these changes as promotions. Typical is one African American midlevel manager in a multinational service corporation who occupied a series of different slots of equivalent status. She believed that she might never, as she put it, "move to a higher level." Conversely, twenty-one of the thirty-one (68 percent) remained at their 1986 title or grade level or moved down. The remainder (three people) made lateral moves out of operations and into support jobs that signaled that, for them, the contest for upward mobility and power was over. All of these executives are on the beach; they have been taken out of the game. A look at the characteristics associated with executives in nonracialized careers shows that both market forces and race are operating to shape the economic future of African American executives.

Placement in Companies

Nearly half the managers in nonracialized careers in 1986 were in personnel-related, public relations, and other support jobs. This pattern is consistent with other surveys, which show that African Americans with executive titles in Chicago's white corporations were not in the profit-driven planning and production jobs that lead to power within organizations (Chicago Urban League 1977). Although support jobs are not racialized, neither do they lie within the corporate loop of power or the mainstream work arena (Kanter 1977). They are peripheral functions with no responsibilities for profits or loss, out of the mainstream route for upward mobility. Only five of twenty-nine managers in this study who made it to the level of vice-president or above specialized in personnel. The remainder were in production, operations, and sales.

White graduates from the country's top business schools (Kellogg, Wharton, Harvard, and Stanford, for example) apparently avoid such support jobs on their road to the top of major companies. Of 1,362 executives with an MBA degree responding to a survey of senior level executives in Fortune 500 Industrial companies and Fortune Service 500 companies only 4 percent started in personnel and just 6 percent were in personnel when the study was conducted (Korn/Ferry 1986). In comparison, in my study 20 percent of non-racialized executives with a graduate degree in business started in personnel, and 30 percent were in personnel when they were interviewed. If racialized careers were included in this profile, the disparity in the occupational outcomes of black and white executives would be even larger. In sum, personnel jobs in this study, but not in studies of successful white executives, represent a sizable proportion of the opportunity structure filled by black men and women deemed to be successful managers. In 1980, African Americans employed in management-related occupations were almost twice as likely as whites to be in a personnel, training, and labor relations job (28 percent versus 15 percent), a proportion that had increased by 1990.

Corporate support areas such as personnel and public relations jobs mirror racialized jobs in a company. Black visibility in personnel and public relations positions is symbolically meaningful to black publics and useful for projecting an image of commitment to racial equality and sensitivity. In the 1980s it was hard for a major employer to justify the absence of black managers in a personnel department, given the overall high concentration of blacks in personnel areas. Individuals in these jobs, however, typically have no budget and few, if any, direct staff reporting to them; they are politically and operationally useful but not critical to an organization, and typically are the least prestigious administrative team members. Operations people, for example, viewed support managers as holding dead-end jobs, that is, out of the running for the top positions. Jackall (1988) notes managers' tendency to characterize the myriad of people in their occupational world, and the phrase "personnel types" was used repeatedly by operations people in my study to characterize personnel workers. "Personnel types have no power" over line managers, noted one, because they tend to lack operating experience. "Personnel types don't want to get their hands dirty," said another line manager, "and basically they're lazy." It is no surprise, then, that recommendations from personnel executives have little credibility with the central core of a company's directors (Kanter 1977). The positions' deficits in corporate power and prestige, in turn, force incumbents to beg to sit at the table where hiring decisions are made.

In sum, the typical African American executive career path, racialized or not, converged in corporate arenas that neutralized their power to change the culture of companies. Although both racialized and nonracialized jobs pushed them a certain distance up the corporate ladder, the jobs offered the least chances to wield influence, control resources, or sustain upward career mobility. White executives view personnel as one of the worst routes to top jobs in a company (Korn/Ferry 1990)—the crumbs at the corporate table.

Where the advancement of African Americans is tied to support functions, as in personnel, further advancement becomes differentially problematic in a rapidly changing economy with periods of job shortages. First, the mobility of African American managers is relatively more limited in corporate settings because of the nature of the jobs in which they are concentrated. Second, when corporate mergers and buyouts displace workers, personnel executives will fare relatively poorly compared to well-educated workers who perform the essential operations at the heart of a company, positions central to a firm's purpose. Workers employed in jobs less central to core operations are easier to discard. Third, support staff may confront a job market whose demand for their talent has diminished. One estimate from out-placement specialists is that displaced managers and professionals in human resources, information resources, and finance and accounting functions take about eight to ten months to find new jobs, compared to about 6.4 months for those in marketing and sales (Whittingham-Barnes 1993). For these reasons, perhaps, placement specialists urge African American executives to move out of support areas, as Jonathan Hicks reported in "Blacks Refashion Their Careers" in the *Wall Street Journal,* 11 November 1985. Knowledgeable insiders view these jobs in the business world as having been hit especially hard over the last several years.

The direct experience of executives I interviewed offers some support for this perspective. One reported that executive heads of support staff were the first positions to go after a company acquisition, while line officers were transferred to the parent company because they had an essential expertise. Another executive experienced a corporate buyout in which most of the officers in support jobs were treated in "quasi-patronage" terms and replaced by the new CEO's own team; line officers were retained. The exception was this African American chief financial officer, who believed his technical expertise (and his likability) prompted the new owner and CEO of the parent company to retain him.

Thus, within the "nonracialized" structure of managerial jobs the division of labor is racially differentiated, with mixed implications for African Americans in the 1990s. On the positive side, because support positions serve a permanent function for employers, unlike the transient role of racialized positions, blacks would be no more likely than whites to absorb the cost of private sector restructuring. On the negative side, support positions, outside the mainstream of companies, are soft roles in a hard environment where the pressure is on individuals to demonstrate a tangible contribution to the corporate bottom line. Performance standards in support jobs like personnel management are tied to subjective rather than to quantified measures, such as profit, sales, or production figures. The profit-generating capacity of personnel jobs would be hard to quantify. In this scenario, the "soft" positions of African American managers in the corporate division of labor would make them more superfluous and gains in these areas relatively more fragile and vulnerable to erosion. Equally negative, African American managers in these jobs are sidetracked from routes to positions of power. Even in the market-spawned (rather than politically spawned) sector of jobs in corporations, they are concentrated in useful but powerless positions.

Downsizing, Flattening, and Affirmative Action

African Americans attribute their career stagnation to processes they associate with corporate downsizing and restructuring, such as the trimming of functions and excess personnel. Some black executive careers are casualties of corporate attempts to meet new competition from domestic and international businesses. For instance, a company once considered the leader in its industry went through a period of flat sales brought on by stiffer competition, followed by several phases of staff reductions, departmental reorganizations, and new standards of profit accountability from middle management. In this process the size of a black executive's staff had been reduced from three people reporting to him in 1986 to one in 1992. Other individuals stagnated because of a relatively new business trend in which hierarchical, vertically integrated corporations are "flattening." In Chicago, for example, one nationally known professional service firm implemented a team-leader strategy, dismantling the hierarchical framework that more typically defines promotions in corporate structures. Such organizational changes make it harder to move up in a company and easier to fail. One executive who had worked for the company for twelve years said, "I don't think I'll make twenty." Nineteen of the fifty nonracialized executives in this study (38 percent) left companies altogether between my first and second interviews and went out on their own.

African American sentiment mirrors that of nonblack managers. The displacement of executives, administrators, and managerial professionals due to cutbacks or plant closings jumped by 50 percent between 1987 and 1992 (U.S. Bureau of Labor Statistics, unpublished tables). In the theoretical framework linking blacks' attainments to political pressure, however, one may plausibly identify the brunt of such changes as inequitably borne by African American executives. The most powerful weapon against bias in administrative hiring and promotion—the OFCC's ability to affect profits based on affirmative-action compliance—was undermined during the 1980s (Leonard 1988), as the agency's use of sanctions, such as back-pay awards and show-cause notices declined sharply, and compliance audits (which doubled between 1979 and 1985) became more perfunctory than critical (Leonard 1984, 1988; Orfield and Ashkinaze 1991).

Slack federal enforcement is compounded by macroeconomic changes to create an environment more lenient about implementing problack employment efforts. With such efforts aimed at now quiescent constituencies, it has become easier to neglect the quest for a more equalitarian society. In a survey of business leaders, for instance, affirmative action appeared far down on the list of business priorities, ranked twenty-third of the top twenty-five human resource management issues (Dingle 1988). Similarly, Hanigan Consulting of New York City found that recruitment of minority college graduates by Fortune 500 companies fell after 1989. Although overall hiring at U.S. campuses was down for the same period, one might have predicted that a greater percentage of minorities would be hired because minority enrollment on college campuses is growing.

Even where affirmative-action goals are implemented, they can be reoriented to recruit nonblack, nonracial, and more politically active minorities. Since the dual political pressures that underpinned blacks' mobility—federal sanctions and black collective action—have receded, blacks predictably would lose ground to other segments of labor. A retired affirmative-action manager noted that his old employer was "once characterized as . . . doing . . . things to help stabilize African American communities, [but now] initiatives are appropriated by other groups or are going away." In a similar vein, in a 14 September 1993 *Wall Street Journal* article, "Losing Ground," Rochelle Sharpe raises the possibility that corporate restructuring of major employers during the 1990–1991 recession disproportionately displaced working-class African Americans, while whites, Hispanics, and Asians gained thousands of jobs. However, Sharpe reported that African Americans' share of managerial, professional, and technical jobs in large corporations, although very small, did not decline.[2]

Between 1980 and 1990 nonracial minorities, such as Hispanics and women, entered managerial occupations at a much faster rate than did African Americans; in the previous decade the reverse trend was true for blacks vis-à-vis other ethnic groups protected by Title VII (Anderton, Barrett, and Bogue forthcoming). One explanation is that 1970s labor markets were shaped by race-conscious activism on the part of blacks and the federal government. After 1980 blacks became much less vocal and politically active, while other groups adopted the political model for status attainment that had served blacks so well, as evidenced by a *Chicago Sun-Times* 12 December 1994 article, "Hispanics Condemn Lack of School Jobs" and other sources (Ramos 1994). Although blacks still made gains in managerial jobs, this trend would explain why, relative to other minorities, their gains are rapidly winding down.

Relative changes in employment distribution are most striking in the progress made by women. Between 1968 and about 1971, the proportion of black men managers only briefly equaled that of white women; from about 1972 onward the proportion of white women managers shot up and rapidly surpassed the black male proportion (Bureau of Labor Statistics n.d.; U.S. Equal Employment Opportunity Commission n.d.). A vice-president of personnel in the financial service industry observed, "If you look at the numbers, there are more white women moving along . . . at a faster rate, than there are African American males. I . . . guess that white women, . . . Hispanics, . . . [and] Asians are closer to him [i.e., white men] in culture . . . [even if] just the texture of hair."

There is no way to know whether hiring, firing, or promotional decisions discriminate against these black executives. Motives that shape job allocations always look ambiguous to people outside the decision-making process. Ultimately, the extent to which employers view fair employment goals as "quotas" and African American workers as "tokens" predicts the shape of blacks' professional and managerial job opportunities in the future. With no race-based legislation or framework for community activism in place, race may once again interact with class to produce the more traditional and discriminatory results.

Gentlemanly Quotas and Glass Ceilings

A group of "heavy hitters" in private industry stood out from the typical pattern because of their positions as corporate officers.[3] Three of the executives I interviewed were chief officers, five were senior vice-presidents in operations, two were vice-presidents in corporate finance, and one was a chief finance officer (CFO). Finance carries exceptionally high status, although it is a support position, because the occupant typically plays a powerful role in a company.

Between 1986 and 1994 the number of this chosen few, already very small, eroded. People once near or at the peak of the job pyramid had ceded their line power in the company or had become self-employed. Each of the three chief officers—the CEO, CFO, and chief operating officer (COO)—were self-employed. Of five senior vice-presidents, two were self-employed, and two had moved into social policy–related areas from core line functions. Further down the pyramid, four of the twelve vice-presidents were self-employed, and two others had moved into support areas.

It was rare for executives in these higher echelons to experience lateral movement or promotions by changing companies. The market is soft for high-level executives, so few who left a company found equivalent or better jobs in the white private sector. Ultimately they started their own businesses.

Reasons for this may be racial in nature. The early 1990s was an employer's market, and the recession of 1990–1991 hit older and white-collar workers. Conventional wisdom holds that corporations seek to hire younger people, a state of affairs that would handicap higher-ranking African American and whites due to age. On the other hand, the market may be soft because the boardrooms of major companies remain all-white bastions of power (Heidrick and

Struggles 1979a, 1979b, 1984). In 1995 there was still not one African American CEO among the Fortune 500 industrial corporations. The only African American, Reginald Lewis, who ever attained that position became the CEO of a billion-dollar firm not by moving up the ladder, anointed by whites, but by buying the company.

Members of a national association of African American executives at officer or equivalent levels in Fortune 1,000 companies across the country reported that, with some exceptions, fellow members seldom leave a company in midstream. Conversely, they perceive that a market exists for similarly situated whites, who achieve promotions by jumping from company to company. Accurate or not, their self-reports reflect the mobility pattern of black Chicago executives. Most with titles of vice-president or higher had reached that level with one employer.[4] Only about 18 percent of 698 white executives working for major employers reported in 1990 that they had worked for only one firm (Korn/Ferry 1990).

Given these top black executives' reemployment records, one questions their chances of capturing equivalent jobs should they fail in one company. An intriguing case among my interviewees is that of the first African American ever to be appointed COO in a Fortune 500 company. In 1986 he indicated no plans either to leave or to start his own business. On the contrary, a popular national business magazine featured him as a major corporate star likely to become the first African American CEO of a Fortune 500 company. Reportedly, however, his eventual exit was connected at least partially to the publicity generated by this article. He left the company, expecting to move laterally to another Fortune 500 company, but reported that he did not receive an acceptable offer. After an extended job search, he left the white private sector altogether.

As the restructuring of the labor market interacts with the fragmentation of blacks' power, their chances of entering the corporate sanctum today monopolized by whites appears even more problematic. Some evidence indicates that blacks did best in companies where we can infer race-conscious intent operating in the background. In 1979 the largest proportion of black senior executives were employed in billion-dollar companies, in firms headquartered in the East, in organizations with the largest work forces, and in consumer products companies (Heidrick and Struggles 1979b). Sizable companies and consumer product companies face a trio of race-related considerations: federal regulatory requirements, public relations, and labor relations. Yet even under relatively supportive political conditions and less uncertainty in the economy, the corporate world enforced a gentlemanly quota on blacks in senior level executive positions. Excluding chief executive officers and presidents, nonwhites constitute less than 1 percent of senior level executives (Korn/Ferry 1986, 1990). White corporations, both nationwide and in Chicago, consistently fail to include senior blacks at these levels beyond token numbers, despite legislative efforts (Chicago Urban League 1977; Heidrick and Struggles 1979a; Korn/Ferry 1986, 1990; Theodore and Taylor 1991).

Corporate Politics and the Comfort Criterion

Political games are played at every level of a company, and "at the top of the pyramid the stakes just get higher," noted one executive, particularly in political battles over who will take the helm of a rapidly changing company. Over time, ascension in the corporate structure means that executives who play well — whether white or black — will move ahead. Those who do not will be moved out or moved aside.

Yet black executives cannot be viewed simply as political players like any others in a competitive corporate culture, for an abundance of research indicates comfort and compatibility as important considerations when incumbents select people to work with and to succeed them (Fernandez 1981; Kanter 1977). The comfort criterion interacts with race and creates another perspective for understanding black executives' standing. An illustrative case concerns one of the most senior executives in the study.

In 1986 this man noted that he didn't want to "seem too boastful" when I asked where he saw himself in the next five years, but he thought he had an excellent chance ("95 percent sure") of being promoted to the next executive level. When a major internal shake-up occurred because profits were falling, the senior executive level was reorganized, some members were reshuffled, and new operating positions were put in place to steer a rapidly changing organization into new national and international markets. Only one person jumped to the next executive level, and that was not the executive I interviewed, who by 1993, seven years after our first talk, appeared more guarded about his future, an executive "on the beach," although this was an image he clearly wished to avoid presenting. In the year following our second interview, he was forced out of operations and moved into diversity, an incongruous shift considering his skills.[5] Apparently a decision had been made to move him aside but not release him from the company.

Selection for advancement in the upper regions of the corporate world rarely hinges solely on the ability to do a job but is connected as well to subjective criteria and the extent work groups believe that each job contender "fits in" (Jackall 1988; Kanter 1977). This subjectivity makes African American people — through color, culture, and sometimes political consciousness — obvious targets of bias in the selection process. A senior executive who left a company to start his own business rather than be passed over continually for promotion said,

> As I went higher in the organization . . . other factors [overshadowed my] performance. I don't think that I was particularly successful in negotiating those factors to my favor. [Question: Other factors?] Well it couldn't have been my performance. I not only met, but I exceeded, my performance goals every year, and many times I was the only person to do so. Your race. Your attitudes. I wasn't politically conservative, and I wasn't too good at hiding that. And on more than one occasion, I developed a feeling that I wasn't being selected for further promotion.

Having gotten "the message," as he put it, he left the company by 1994. At least in his own eyes the talents and skills that had until then sustained his mobility became irrelevant when he stood one job away from the company's inner circle. Objective performance goals were overshadowed by subjective dynamics that help people to feel at ease. He left the company when he realized he would never be "picked by someone and brought to their table."

Neither differences in appearance nor a wide range of other differences are easily tolerated in the ranks of managers (Jackall 1988; Kanter 1977). African Americans contending against whites for power are both isolates and tokens. Race-related stereotypes and dissimilarities heightened by tokenism are likely to emerge (Kanter 1977). Race becomes a wild card easily played against them, particularly in the competition for jobs involving uncertainty in which stereotypes and tradition work against exotic workers (Kanter 1977; Pfeffer 1982). Corporate slots rarely held by African Americans have been relinquished by them — and filled by whites.

Apart from race, tokenism of any kind hinders one's ability to form the political coalitions necessary to win out against contenders for top jobs. Blacks must be adept at forming coalitions across racial lines, which is exceedingly hard to do. Furthermore, the dominant group becomes alert to token individuals, a heightened awareness that accentuates differences (Kanter 1977). Historically, the exaggeration of racial differences in particular has caused those differences to become devalued and inequality rationalized. I know of only one person who has successfully transcended race on his journey to the top of a white-dominated bureaucracy, the former head of the Joint Chiefs of Staff, Colin Powell.

Marginal Men

At the same time executives must be selected by others to move up, they must adapt themselves to fit in. For black executives, successful adaptation undermines racial cohesion and racial group solidarity, creating marginal men and women with one foot in each racial culture who belong to neither.

African American managers were outsiders in all-white institutions in the 1970s, unwanted participants in a socially and racially homogeneous occupation, who survived and thrived more by consciously conforming and submerging racial differences than by aggressive individualism. The beached executive who held the highest rank of those I interviewed, for example, succeeded in a white culture where loyalty and commitment to the company, and total adherence to company norms, are highly valued. He was reminiscent of the "other-directed" corporate man of the 1950s who followed a safe path, looked good, and made no waves (Fromm 1955; Harrington 1959; Mills 1951; Riesman 1950; Whyte 1956). Repeatedly he mentioned that he would do what it took to "serve the company." He used the word "we" (referring to himself and the company) continually, creating and reinforcing my perception that he was a company man, a team player, an image that had surely helped him get ahead.

The role conformity played in black executives getting ahead becomes more clear in the vocabularies of people with titles of vice-presidents and above compared to those of lower-ranked executives. Higher-ranked executives were generally less likely to distinguish themselves in racial terms during our interview. They had, for example, a greater tendency to speak of the company using terms such as "family," and to use inclusive terms such as "we" and "us" rather than "they" and "them." Fewer of their references to white peers and superiors or to career routes could be construed as criticism. Overall, they were much less likely to frame their understanding of their careers in racial terms. The most senior executives in this study had internalized a norm that called for demonstrating loyalty, treating even the privacy of our interview as a chance to demonstrate color-blindness, company commitment, and social conformity.

As blacks in a white world their survival and success relied, at least to some degree, on being "nonblack" to win white acceptance. In order to succeed, that is, this vanguard of blacks minimized conflict, didn't make waves, and avoided controversy. For African Americans, but not for whites, fitting into the bureaucratic culture means shedding the racial self and submerging racial history and differences. The corporate world is, after all, an environment where one gains advantages from interpersonal relationships. Put another way, these managers' success in the conservative world of large corporations requires that they gloss over potentially volatile differences where race matters.

The marginal run the risk of being perceived as outsiders — that is, culturally and politically suspect — by generalized others in the black community. One very high-ranking executive was characterized by lower-ranking blacks as the company's "fair-haired boy" who symbolized a degree of co-optation and communal betrayal. His strategies for moving ahead were provocative to these blacks; they viewed him as isolated from other African Americans in the company and as attempting to "fit in with whites" and to garner white approval. This executive also was summed up as a person who had put himself in "an awfully lonesome spot [vis-à-vis other blacks in the company] for an awfully long time." Other blacks in the company demeaned him because, I was told, "he became someone who didn't remember where he came from."

Executives who didn't have, develop, or keep a black constituency that would come forward when their jobs were threatened decreased their power base. In the 1960s, pressure from black constituencies created new opportunities that these executives exploited. In the 1990s, the lack of a constituency means these executives can be treated like any other member of the team, but with vastly different group consequences. The "fair-haired boy" just described represented a dramatic measure of black gain. Between our first and second interview he was promoted from vice-president of operations to company president. But he had no black constituency to call on later to protest his firing from that position. In 1995 this once high-powered man was without a job. If blacks' racial group solidarity is splintered by the process of upward mobility, the capacity of the group is undermined.

Overall, it is doubtful that the federally mandated race-based employment programs that began in the 1960s ever were intended to be a permanent part of the legislative landscape. The hope instead, it would seem, was that the proximity, the influence, and the achievements of African Americans would deracialize the cultures of employment and achievement. The movement of employers toward a color-blind posture in hiring and promotion would take on a life of its own. Thus, from the point of progress, it was — and still is — good news that most African American executives who participated in this study in 1986 did not occupy race-specified roles in Chicago corporations. Finding them employed outside the corporate niche of politically mediated jobs was a positive forecast for the continued integration of African Americans throughout the private sector. Perhaps race-based job allocation in the postindustrial economy *can* give way to race-blind fair employment policies. Perhaps this competitive African American executive elite *can* protect and reproduce its position via human capital and business networks, without federal protections.

However, labor market restructuring increases competitiveness along lines drawn by race, gender, ethnicity, and ideology inside the culture. At the same time, the significance of net gains or net loss in the job market and downward mobility for each race and ethnic group are hardly equal, a concept essential for recognizing discriminatory processes in a labor market context.[6] That is, even if equal numbers of African Americans and whites lose jobs, the impact on the aggregate status of African Americans would be relatively much greater. The progress made since the 1960s could be seriously undermined.

Chapter 9

Bursting the Bubble: The Failure of Black Progress

✦ Most scholars agree that dramatic progress was made in blacks' access to white-collar occupations over the past three decades. One explanation points to the forces of an impersonal labor market that rewarded improvements in black skills and education with occupational mobility in a growing service economy (see Smith and Welch 1978b). And, indeed, both aggregate data and individual cases show that college-educated blacks improved their position when the economy was on the upswing and the need for skilled labor was expanding.

Yet the timing of blacks' attainment as revealed by my study, in conjunction with other research (such as Freeman 1976a; Leonard 1984), strongly links this attainment to political pressures on employers exerted by government and by the black community. Since black executives in Chicago entered the job market in an environment dominated by black political activism and governmental intervention, I suggested that the elaboration of the black middle class that has been attributed to their entry into higher-paying white-collar jobs is not grounded solely in their educational attainments and in economic trends. The growing demand for blacks in higher-paying jobs is also a function of a shift in hiring to conform to blacks' demands for increased access to economic resources and to government regulations. I do not mean that education, skills, and related factors such as motivation and hard work are trivial to blacks' gains and greater competitiveness. I mean, rather, that blacks' objective qualifications are still strongly intertwined with racialized processes that continue to operate in the labor market.

Before the 1960s the market economy that spawned the black middle class was dominated by artificial and race-based barriers, not free and impersonal exchange. It was an economy shaped by restrictions that limited interaction between the races and that allowed black business and professional opportunities only in the segregated environment of black ghettos. This economy created opportunities in a narrow range of service areas for a very small number of blacks, such as doctors, morticians, and lawyers. The opportunity structure was broadened somewhat when blacks were able to enter the public sector as teachers or other professionals. But even this somewhat broadened economic system was structured along racial lines: Black professionals distributed services to other blacks, as opposed to the total (i.e., predominantly white) community.

These race-linked occupational restrictions are reflected in executives' descriptions of their labor market experiences. Most college-trained blacks entering the labor market before 1965 went to work for the government. Only the most highly educated broke into the professions in the white private sector. Even in these cases, characteristics ascribed to a free market were not in play; they worked almost exclusively in industries that depended heavily on government contracts for survival.

From the mid-1960s onward, the labor market for educated blacks underwent a transformation. College-educated blacks entered the economic mainstream in jobs similar to those of their white counterparts that better reflected their training and abilities. It appeared that artificial racial barriers had lifted as college-educated blacks captured the incomes and occupations to support the middle-class life-styles previously reserved for whites. For the first time in history, the structure of opportunity for college-educated blacks shifted significantly to include higher-paying white-collar jobs in the central economy.

My study documents this shift in executives' reports of job search experiences, which showed a much broader spectrum of jobs available to them after the mid-1960s than before. After 1965 their rate for going into sales jobs tied to unstable black consumer sectors and into low-paying clerical positions decreased by two-thirds. At the same time, at the other end of the white-collar job spectrum, twice the proportion had access to professional and managerial jobs in the white private sector. Overall, these changes in patterns of employment are consistent with other research showing that the socioeconomic status of blacks jumped dramatically when college-educated blacks entered professional-managerial jobs inside government and private industry.

My study reflects the increase in compliance pressures on the part of the EEOC and the OFCCP at the same time that managerial and professional job opportunities in white organizations increased. Executives entering business-related fields credited the activism of black organizations and civil disturbances with helping to create their job opportunities; two-thirds of them who entered business-related fields after 1965 knew of the vulnerability of their company to black consumer boycotts and the vulnerability of company property to urban upheaval, and three-quarters of this group also knew that their employment was a result of a company effort to hire blacks.

Further evidence of a connection between political variables and black employment opportunities appears in employment patterns where blacks fill jobs mediating black demands for white institutions. That is, the alchemy of market and political forces not only influenced new behavior on the part of employers, it also increased demand for blacks by increasing social service and manpower development programs in government and in private industry. Although blacks clearly made gains in a variety of jobs, the new black middle class is grounded in professional and business roles created or reoriented to nullify pressure from black people.

A sizable majority of African American managers in the upper echelons of Chicago's white corporations were channeled into an occupational structure that evolved from the pressures of the civil rights period. Two-thirds of those I interviewed had held at least one job that was oriented toward blacks over the course of their private sector career. One-third of the managers were concentrated in race-oriented jobs throughout their career. This nascent business elite moved, in particular, into personnel areas of corporations to administer affirmative-action policies and into public relations areas to respond to turbulent black communities. One-third of the managers I interviewed who entered the white private sector after 1965 were recruited to fill jobs in one of these two areas; others were enticed to transfer into these jobs by salary increases, better job titles, and promises of future rewards. Even those with incompatible backgrounds and highly technical skills — such as accountants, engineers, and chemists — were tracked into affirmative-action and public relations areas. The forces expanding blacks' economic opportunities were protest related, and the new black middle class is at least in part a politically mediated phenomenon.

My portrayal of the black middle class is both consistent with and different from the dominant theoretical perspectives on race and labor markets. While I agree that unprecedented advancement occurred within the black middle class, I do not agree that attainment among blacks is evidence of the deracialization of labor markets (cf. Wilson 1978). Middle-class attainments among blacks reflect a dependence on employment practices that are sensitive to race. Better job opportunities for blacks are connected to federal legislation and to the expansion of social service bureaucracy and other administrative apparatuses to implement social policies designed to appease disruptive black constituencies.

My observations of the characteristics of jobs that blacks hold contradict the notion that spontaneous market demands in tandem with education and skill lifted the employment barriers faced by talented blacks. Such qualifications are necessary, but they have never been sufficient to ensure the relative success of blacks in the economy. Governmental mandates — not the forces of free markets — are critical to expand and stabilize the black middle class.

Finally, my findings go beyond research that highlights the effects of affirmative-action kinds of government policy on the black middle class to indicate that the intent of such policy is not assimilated by the marketplace. An analysis of the careers of highly successful black executives with great potential as competitors inside the mainstream labor market showed that the economy opened up in only a distinctive and marginalized way. Private employers channeled a group of people with a variety of talent into racialized careers during the 1960s and 1970s. Even the majority of mainstream, that is, non-racialized, careers found in this group have marginalized features. Executives in this study are concentrated in support areas where institutional objectives reflect policy attempts to nullify blacks' potential for disruption, not in the planning and operations functions oriented toward profit that lead to power in an organization. My view of the black middle class is consistent with a conflict model of class relations rather than with traditional status attainment models. Blacks' advancement is a function of protest, and this protest was not resolved by true deracialization in the labor market. Rather, the role of race has been reconfigured in the modern economy and continues to have an impact on blacks' access to middle-class positions.

Implications for Racial Equality

What do a politically mediated model and racialized jobs have to say about blacks' chances for economic equality? The short answer is that they are not likely to eradicate inequality.

In the scenario of this book, demand is mediated by an interrelationship among economic upswings, political pressures, and a labor supply of qualified workers. The intersection of these three factors created the conditions for some blacks to rise and compete for higher-paying jobs against whites. Yet the processes of attainment reported here show that blacks' new socioeconomic status does not necessarily indicate racial equality in institutions or in labor markets. First, some types of racial segregation and economic inequality are maintained and even facilitated by the mechanisms associated with black middle-class mobility. Second, if the black middle class results from special political and legal conditions, then it can be argued that it occupies a fragile economic position.

Maintaining Inequality

Since the mid-1960s, the black middle class no longer has been relegated strictly to the lower ends of occupation and income hierarchies or restricted by geography. However, a new structure of inequality was created by a system of employment opportunities that channeled some blacks into racialized functions. On the positive side, this system of jobs afforded some blacks a chance to succeed economically and garner unprecedented, albeit temporary, status in white institutions. The negative half of the equation is that this system could not solve the problem of blacks in the long run. Affirmative-action managers, for instance, wrote hiring plans and were in charge of their implementation. But affirmative action was implemented with an eye toward appeasing governmental and public relations requirements, not changing the color of power brokers in white institutions. Data show that black men in particular are underrepresented—even after thirty years of affirmative-action efforts—in managerial jobs and in almost every business-related profession.

Progress was limited because the incumbents of racialized jobs simply did not have the power to change institutional practices. The ability to get things done required access to and persuasiveness with the CEO and other top management. Executives I interviewed who survived in these roles were not individuals likely to risk their jobs by "pushing the envelope" and disrupting the equilibrium of their employing institution. It is logical to presume that they survived in these jobs because of their ability to accommodate whites, not embarrass the company, and not cause trouble.

Their jobs helped companies conform to federal regulations, and programmatic allocations (such as technical assistance, corporate funding of community-based projects and job training) both quelled urban pressures and undermined claims of racism, creating a progressive, more socially conscious, corporate image. But these allocations were too small and were viewed by companies as a short-term atonement for past grievances, rather than as a long-term commitment to justice. Racialized jobs, therefore, were instrumental in negotiating the needs of the black community and in distributing corporate resources, but they ultimately maintained inequality by temporarily abating black pressures and meanwhile marginalizing the incumbent.

At the same time, this study makes it clear that racialized jobs effectively kept their incumbents from traveling conventional routes up the corporate ladder. When individuals in this study entered race-oriented and staff positions in white companies, they assumed career tracks that typically do not lead to line power in a company. Once in these jobs, many of them were constrained by the perception or the reality that they lacked the necessary skills to contribute in a mainstream function. Consequently, gains they made over the last three decades did not — and will not — blossom into meaningful numbers of executives heading production and planning areas. The tracks their careers took in the 1960s and 1970s diminished the pool of blacks in Chicago corporations who could compete to manage mainstream production units in the 1980s and beyond.

In sum, managers in this study are part of a black middle class that has occupied a useful but nonadversarial position in white companies. Ultimately this means that racialized jobs were a factor in reducing competition for power in organizations along racial lines. And, since they were unable to succeed in policy- and decision-making positions in meaningful numbers, it is doubtful that the makeup or resource allocation of organizations will change dramatically. Even current policy decisions to continue affirmative-action programs are contested outside any arena in which blacks exercise power.

What I have found, therefore, is a structure of achievement that preserved inequality while it carried out its role in reinstating social order, and that established a class position with obsolete features built in. Executives in this study were desirable candidates for affirmative-action and public relations jobs at a time of intense social upheaval; when pressure from blacks abated, the status of many of these executives tumbled. Specifically, as racial pressures were ameliorated in Chicago, racialized jobs lost their value. Given the relationship between these jobs and the political pressures faced by white corporations during the 1960s and 1970s, one could take the position that affirmative-action and urban affairs managers did their jobs for companies too well. In relieving the pressure on companies, they not only helped shut the window of opportunity through which other blacks could follow but they undermined the very element that had produced their own positions.

African American Middle-Class Fragility

Although job opportunities for college-educated blacks and whites have converged since the 1960s, class mobility for these two groups stems from different factors. In my view of black attainment, the opportunity to earn income and maintain middle-class life-styles depended as heavily on blacks' broad social status and the activity of the state apparatus as on general economic trends. First, African Americans were viewed by major employers as desirable candidates for professional and managerial jobs because of governmental sanctions. Second, meeting the needs of, or solving, the problems of blacks was near the top of the public policy agenda.

Extending this view leads to the conclusion that different factors insure the economic viability of blacks and whites. Thus, if the federal government dismantles strong race-specific programs and affirmative-action mandates, employer effort to create and maintain equal employment opportunities may shrink accordingly. Indeed, this study suggests that the institutional mechanisms for protecting black attainments in the white private sector — affirmative-action and community relations departments — *are* shrinking and becoming watered down. Weakening these areas weakens the race-conscious influence on employment decisions that in the past protected blacks. Moreover, departures from the liberal social thinking that dominated Congress in the 1960s make likely a radically different political agenda and an alteration in the basis for federal policy and spending decisions.

The federal government's incentives and sanctions in the 1960s and the 1970s were not meant to change the intrinsic nature of the economy but only to get employers to respond differently. Two outcomes are possible if these incentives and sanctions are dismantled. First, despite race-conscious political supports, blacks' qualifications and the greater acceptance of blacks in white-dominated settings may enable the same or a larger relative proportion of blacks to move further up the economic ladder. Or, second, the proportion of employed blacks in the next cohort to enter higher-paying white-collar occupations may erode. In the first outcome we would see significant further progress in the black middle class in capturing positions of power within white institutions. In the second outcome, we would see stagnation or vastly diminished rates of change.

Of these two options, the second, I believe, is the more plausible. The link between black class mobility and political pressure predicts the fragility of the middle-class position. Although black protest and government intervention theoretically occur outside the market-place, they are two of the three ingredients necessary for blacks' economic progress. That is, the status of the economy, the level of black activism, and the public policy agenda all assisted blacks to rise. I believe that gains made in the black middle class will dissolve in the next generation of labor force participants for reasons related to all three of these ingredients.

Changes in Public Policy

The race-based legislation and spending that assisted blacks to rise is being challenged and dismantled. As a general proposition, as government funding dwindles from social service areas and federal efforts abate in employment legislation, the ability of blacks to maintain and to continue their gains will also erode. If federal antibias employment policy and government spending in social service arenas created the conditions that opened up nontraditional white-collar jobs to blacks, it follows that cutbacks in affirmative-action programs in major companies and cutbacks in government social services would decrease the demand for blacks in specified occupations.

In the national debate, some social critics see blacks' dependence on government as a negative outcome of federal protections. However, I see government dependency as an unavoidable partner in blacks' progress. Because the federal government did not change the intrinsic nature of the economy or of employers, equal employment and color-blind hiring are not institutionalized in the labor market, and fair employment practices would not continue in the government's absence. We must think of affirmative action not only as reparation for past discrimination but also as an instrument necessary to prevent present acts of employment discrimination. And there is plenty of evidence to indicate that racial discrimination, both economic and social, still exists (Cose 1993; Feagin and Sikes 1994; Jones 1986; Kirschenman and Neckerman 1991; Massey and Denton 1993; U.S. Department of Housing and Urban Development 1991).

Black Power Versus Passivity

Within a politically mediated model of middle-class ascendancy, black gains may be fragile for another reason. The rise of the new black middle class is tied to black collective action, but splintered interests and large economic divisions now exist within the black community. In the 1950s, class divisions existed, but segregation forged a racial group consciousness that, in the face of white terrorism, transcended factionalism based on occupational and income differences.[1] In the 1990s, however, the gap caused by the assimilation of a skilled and highly educated black middle class and the dislocation and exclusion of a black underclass may mean that blacks have less ability to form alliances and harness the power of collective action.

The emergence of the new black middle class and blacks' new forms of institutional participation, in part, occurred by siphoning activists and future leaders out of the black community. This siphoning process mirrors that which William Wilson (1987) describes when arguing that desegregation spurred the exodus of middle-class blacks from inner-city neighborhoods. Chicago alderman Bobby Rush, former head of the Black Panther Party, and Chief Justice Thurgood Marshall, the NAACP's chief legal strategist for ending segregation in the South, are prominent individual examples. Much less prominent but still relevant examples are managers in this study who, during the 1960s, were community activists with networks that made them useful recruits for manpower training and development jobs in white corporations. They left behind a dispirited black community increasingly beset by social and economic problems.

At the same time, a new type of black accommodationism and white paternalism emerged. As the new black middle class became dependent on whites for jobs, the raised arms with clenched fists associated with "black power" and solidarity that dominated the 1960s were dropped and sleeved among the middle class in the grey flannel associated with being a "company man" and "fitting in." Integration of this black middle-class vanguard into white corporations set it upon a path of achievement and upward mobility that, having separated it from the black collective, also divests it of both the license and the constituency to argue group claims. Nathan Hare once observed that a vanguard detached from the mass becomes an elite. This reasoning, perhaps, allows whites and black neoconservatives disingenuously to dismiss, as a means to exploit race for its own thinly veiled interests, black middle-class complaints about racial barriers.

The problem blacks confront is whether to attempt to go all the way into the system or to go back to their roots. Assimilation has given rise to a new set of community problems without a corresponding rise in economic power. Put another way, the dilemma is whether to continue to pursue the assimilationist goals embodied by traditional civil rights organizations such as PUSH, the Urban League, and the NAACP or to embrace the separatist ideology exemplified by the Black Muslims.

I predict one of two outcomes. In a politically mediated middle class, when racial pressures on white employers emerged, the system of racialized jobs enabled white bureaucracies to mediate the goals and options open to black communities. If black solidarity, filtered through white bureaucracies, grows weaker, then the power of protest blacks exercised three decades ago is weakened also. African Americans would then find it hard to organize protest strategies on a level impressive enough to protect and provoke further economic gains. Under these conditions advancement among middle-class blacks will erode in the future.

In an alternate scenario, having been exposed to education and the subjective philosophy of merit, the black middle class may become more race conscious. Black executives who played by the rules of the game and now confront glass ceilings may become an angry, alienated middle class that gives birth to new and radicalized black leadership. The broad coalition of disparate organizations that supported the 1995 March on Washington and the antipathy that cuts across class lines against denouncing Louis Farrakhan may cue future coalitions. Limitations to black power inside the system may radicalize the black middle class and spur race-based challenges to institutional practices.

The Status of the Economy

Finally, blacks gains will erode because of macroeconomic factors. As companies continue to prune functions and excess personnel to be more competitive, and as a global economy and technological advancements sweep away layers of middle managers, the economic positions of both whites and blacks grow more fragile.

Even in the best of times, when the economy is expanding and good jobs are plentiful, blacks make gains but continue to trail their white counterparts. For example, despite the advancement of black men in managerial and business-related professions, they remain greatly underrepresented in jobs at the core of white corporate America. Forecasts of the status of blacks become even gloomier when one considers the predictable effects of economic recessions. That is, in a soft economy, the competition for jobs that secure middle-class lifestyles stiffens. Indeed, this may be a reason that race-based employment legislation finds little support among whites, as the *Pollwatcher Letter* columnist suggested in the *New York Times* on 12 May 1992. Thus, while both races are affected by restructuring in the marketplace, the risk, the meaning, and the impact differ considerably for blacks and whites.

In the final analysis, using Christian morality and street militancy to provoke white guilt and embarrassment no longer works. First, these strategies depended in large part on shock value, the contrast between American ideals of justice and equality and the reality of blacks' daily existence, particularly in the South. That contrast alone was powerful enough to give black leadership the moral authority to challenge the economic status quo. Now the degree of poverty among African Americans is no longer shocking, in part because what once was hidden beneath the image of America as a middle-class society now is obvious in urban ghettos. Nor is there national sympathy for the claims of blacks. When race-based demonstrations and appeals arise, they are more likely to provoke disdain in whites, to raise the question, What do those people want from us anyway?

Second, the onus of guilt over what went wrong has shifted. Blame once borne by the national conscience has been placed by economic and cultural conservatives on the poor and "undeserving" blacks doomed by white presumptions of inherent black immorality. Dooming them also is the political expediency of using blacks as scapegoats in an era of economic uncertainty. What remnants of guilt remain have been cleansed away by the rise of a black middle class, and by whites' sense of cultural sacrifice and racial beneficence for implementing thirty years of social welfare programs and affirmative action.

Thus, the controversy once tempered by compassion that began with the passage of the Civil Rights Act in 1964 and with affirmative action has reemerged full blown. Widespread public sentiment among whites increasingly rejects the notion of government intervention, according to a *New York Times* Pollwatcher Letter on 12 May 1992. Given the results of the 1995 congressional elections, it also appears that the white electorate now rejects leaders who have a tradition of supporting black causes. This public resentment appears to bring with it a different political climate for the 1990s and perhaps beyond in which whites' political pressure demands that protective policies oriented toward blacks be retracted and allowed to erode.

As a society we seem to disdain history. We ignore the intransigence, the meaning, and the magnitude of racial inequality, thereby making it easier for social critics to trivialize the need for affirmative action. Ahistorical assessments of the impact of antibias employment legislation, moreover, fail to recognize the potential for future racial conflict in the United States. If affirmative action and other race-specific legislation are dismantled, no mechanisms exist to replace them. Affirmative action has always been a hotly contested and controversial policy. It was implemented as a last step in a series of escalating antibias policies because racial strife threatened the fabric of the country and because the mechanisms for racial separation in the core economy are tough and enduring.

NOTES

Chapter 1

1. The term *underclass* designates a heterogeneous grouping at the very bottom of the economic class hierarchy that includes low-paid workers whose income falls below the poverty level, the long-term unemployed, workers who have dropped out of the labor market, and permanent welfare recipients. The heads of households in the underclass are primarily women. Men are primarily unattached and transient. In this definition I am borrowing heavily from the work of William Wilson (1981:21).

2. See, for example, Leonard (1984) and Heckman and Payner (1989) for research on the effects of federal contract compliance programs.

3. One person declined to be interviewed; ten others were not interviewed because of logistical reasons or because they did not meet my criteria.

4. I was able to update information on all the original executives in the study, locating seventy-four of seventy-six and interviewing fifty-nine. Of the seventeen not interviewed, six had moved out of state, two had left a company and could not be located, seven failed to respond to my request for a follow-up interview, and two had died.

Chapter 2

1. Smith and Welch (1986) examined the occupational attainments of the black middle class and argue that upward mobility among blacks preceded the civil-rights legislation of the 1960s. In addition, earlier discussions of federal antibias regulations suggest that the legislation had minimal effects (Adams 1972; Flanagan 1976; Ornati and Pisano 1972; Wolkinson 1973).

2. For comprehensive discussions of affirmative-action and equal employment opportunity programs see Benokraitis and Feagin (1978), Hausman et al. (1977), and Nathan (1969).

3. No data on the percent of federal government procurement going to minority businesses have been published since about 1982.

4. See Brown and Erie (1981) for discussion of the number and source of jobs created in the public sector between 1960 and 1976; see Betsey (1982) on the growth of the public sector between 1939 and 1981.

Chapter 3

1. See Isaac and Kelly (1981) for an analysis of the riot-welfare relationship.

Chapter 4

1. Due to strict segregation in the educational system, black college students were then heavily concentrated in black colleges.

2. *Griggs v. Duke Power* required that if employment tests were shown to have an adverse impact on protected groups, the firm must demonstrate that the test is job related; employers have found it difficult to do so (Burstein and Pitchford 1990; Kirschenman and Neckerman 1991).

3. In identifying the stages, groups, and activities of the civil rights movement I borrow heavily from earlier research and scholarship: Bloom (1987), Sitkoff (1981), Broderick and Meier (1971), and the Civil Rights Education Project of the Southern Poverty Law Center.

4. In one week in June 1963, the Justice Department cited several hundred demonstrations taking place not only in southern cities such as Tallahassee, Savannah, and Jackson, but also in the North, in Providence, Columbus, New York City, and Los Angeles (White 1964).

5. Brand names are deleted because these products are identified with producer and thus might break the executive's anonymity.

6. In 1964, riots erupted first in Harlem, then in Brooklyn, Bedford-Stuyvesant, Rochester, and New York City, and later in Jersey City and Philadelphia. In the summer of 1965, riots broke out in the black ghetto of Watts and in Chicago and San Diego. In 1966, more than two dozen cities were struck by riots; in 1967, Detroit experienced the largest and the most destructive of the series of urban upheavals; and in 1968, waves of rioting followed the assassination of Martin Luther King, Jr.

Chapter 6

1. Set up by the Department of Labor, PICs consisted of local businesses and minority entrepreneurs working with the private and public sector

to identify ways in which private enterprise could take advantage of existing Department of Labor initiatives to increase employment in targeted areas.

2. Under the bonus plan in this company, an employee earned a percentage of the net profit: 1 percent of the first $50,000, 2 percent of the second $50,000, 3 percent of the next, and 4.5 percent of anything over $150,000 in profits. This man reported being "one of the few managers who got in that fourth category."

Chapter 7

1. *Memphis Firefighters v. Stotts* (1984), *Wygant v. Jackson Board of Education* (1986) and *J. A. Croson Company v. City of Richmond* (1989) are examples of key decisions that undermined the principle of racial preferences in employment.

2. In 1986 the Supreme Court in *Local 93 v. City of Cleveland* held that local courts can approve settlements that involve the preferential hiring of blacks. In the same year, the decision in *Local 28 v. Equal Employment Opportunity Commission* approved a lower-court order requiring a union local to hire a fixed quota of blacks.

3. Information conflicts about what in particular happened to managerial jobs during the 1980s. Contrary evidence suggests that black managers are the least likely among workers to lose their jobs in companies during periods of economic distress and that black managers increasingly have been victims of job loss in major corporations.

4. In the 1990s, I found twenty-six executives (100 percent) relocated in segregated careers and interviewed nineteen. I also found forty-nine of the fifty executives (98 percent) in nonracialized careers and interviewed thirty-nine.

Chapter 8

1. Large corporate mergers have somewhat complicated the concept of changing employers, as corporations sometimes become operating divisions of the buying unit. For instance, a vice-president of finance in 1986 worked for a firm that by 1993 was acquired by a larger company, itself a division of a multinational electronics corporation. If individuals were employed in some part of either the old or new entities in this exchange, I viewed them as remaining with their employers. Conversely, I viewed individuals no longer

with their original employers, in whatever form those entities now exist, as leaving their employers.

2. Sharpe's analysis is based on a matched sample of private companies reporting to the EEOC. The U.S. Bureau of Labor Statistics study of 1990–1991 employment data, focused on aggregate level data, found that blacks and whites both suffered a net job loss in this period.

3. Individuals at the corporate officer level are elected by a company's board of directors and generally include the chief executive officer (CEO), chief operating officer, chief financial officer, chief information officer, and the executive vice-presidents of manufacturing, sales, marketing, legal, and human resources. Other executives, appointed at the discretion of the CEO, generally include division presidents and vice-presidents. Consequently, an enlightened CEO can have a significant impact on the racial makeup of senior corporate positions. However, the full board of directors ultimately determines who sits in the corporation's inner circle.

4. Three of twenty-nine vice-presidents or higher entered the first or second tier of a corporate hierarchy by changing companies, recruited in the pre-Reagan years when my theory of a politically mediated labor market would predict a greater demand for African Americans at the executive level.

5. I characterize the move as forced because it was not consistent with what this manager had planned for career advancement. Moreover, he was fully aware that affirmative-action and related jobs are, as he put it, "dead-end jobs [with] no power."

6. There are two ways to prove discrimination in the labor market. The first is by showing disparate *treatment* and the second is by showing disparate *impact*. See Lazaar (1991) for a straightforward account of what constitutes labor market discrimination.

Chapter 9

1. See Bloom (1987) for a perceptive analysis of the emergence of new civil rights leadership in the South.

REFERENCES

Adams, Arvil V. 1972. *Toward Fair Employment and the E.E.O.C.: A Study of Compliance under Title VII of the Civil Rights Act of 1969.* Washington, D.C.: Equal Employment Opportunity Commission.

Allen, Robert L. 1970. *Black Awakening in Capitalist America: An Analytic History.* Garden City, N.Y.: Doubleday.

Althauser, Robert P. 1975. *Unequal Elites.* New York: Wiley.

Ames, Charles B., and James D. Hlavacek. 1989. *Market Driven Management: Prescriptions for Survival in a Turbulent World.* Homewood, N.J.: Dow Jones–Irwin.

Anderton, Douglas L., Richard E. Barrett, and Donald J. Bogue. Forthcoming. *The Population of the United States.*

Ashenfelter, Orley, and James J. Heckman. 1976. "Measuring the Effect of an Anti-discrimination program." In *Evaluating the Labor Market Effects of Social Programs,* ed. O. Ashenfelter and J. Blum, 46–89. Princeton: Industrial Relations Section, Princeton University.

Becker, Brian, and Stephen Hills. 1979. "Today's Teenage Unemployed–Tomorrow's Working Poor?" *Monthly Labor Review* 102 (January): 69–71.

Becker, Gary. 1981. *A Treatise on the Family.* Cambridge: Harvard University Press.

Belohlav, James A., and Eugene Ayton. 1982. "Equal Opportunity Law: Some Common Problems." *Personnel Journal* 61: 282–285.

Benokraitis, Nijole V., and Joe Feagin. 1978. *Affirmative Action and Equal Opportunity.* Boulder: Westview.

Betsey, Charles. 1982. *Minority Participation in the Public Sector.* Washington, D.C.: Urban Institute Press.

Bloom, Jack M. 1987. *Class, Race, and the Civil Rights Movement.* Bloomington: Indiana University Press.

Blumberg, Paul. 1980. *Inequality in the Age of Decline.* New York: Oxford University Press.

Branch, Shelly. 1993. "America's Most Powerful Black Executives." *Black Enterprise,* February, 79–134.

Brimmer, Andrew. 1976. "The Economic Position of Black Americans." *Special Report to the National Commission for Manpower Policy.* No. 9. Washington, D.C.: Commission for Manpower.

Broderick, Francis L., and August Meier. 1971. "Black Protest Thought in the Twentieth Century." Ed. August Meier, Elliott Rudwick, and Francis L. Broderick. 2d. ed. Indianapolis: Bobbs-Merrill.

Brown, Michael K., and Steven P. Erie. 1981. "Blacks and the Legacy of the Great Society: The Economic and Political Impact of Federal Social Policy." *Public Policy* 29 (Summer): 299–330.

Burstein, Paul. 1985. *Discrimination, Jobs, and Politics: The Struggle for Equal Employment Opportunity in the United States Since the New Deal.* Chicago: University of Chicago Press.

Burstein, Paul, and Susan Pitchford. 1990. "Social-Scientific and Legal Challenges to Education and Test Requirements in Employment." *Social Problems* 37 (May): 243–257.

Chicago United. 1980. *Chicago United Compendium of Minority Professional Service Firms.* Chicago: Chicago United.

Chicago Urban League. 1977. *Blacks in Policy-Making Positions in Chicago.* Chicago: Chicago Urban League.

Clark, Kenneth B. 1965. *Dark Ghetto: Dilemmas of Social Power.* New York: Harper and Row.

Cohn, Jules. 1975. "Is Business Meeting the Challenge of Urban Affairs?" *Equal Opportunity in Business.* Harvard Review Reprint Series, no. 21132.

Collins, Sharon M. 1983. "The Making of the Black Middle Class." *Social Problems* 30 (April): 369–382.

Colton, Elizabeth O. 1989. *The Jackson Phenomenon: The Man, the Power, the Message.* New York: Doubleday.

Cose, Ellis. 1993. *The Rage of a Privileged Class: Why Are Middle-Class Blacks Angry? Why Should America Care?* New York: HarperCollins.

Davis, George, and Glegg Watson. 1982. *Black Life in Corporate America: Swimming in the Mainstream.* New York: Doubleday.

Dingle, Derek. 1988. "Will Black Managers Survive Corporate Downsizing?" *Black Enterprise,* March, 51.

Donovan, J. C. 1967. *The Politics of Poverty.* New York: Pegasus.

Drake, St. Clair, and Horace R. Cayton. 1962. *Black Metropolis.* Vol. 2. New York: Harper and Row.

Dreyfuss, Joel, and Charles Lawrence III. 1979. *The Bakke Case: The Politics of Inequality.* New York: Harcourt, Brace, Jovanovich.

Eccles, Mary. 1975. "Race, Sex, and Government Jobs: A Study of Affirmative Action Programs in Federal Agencies." Ph.D. diss., Harvard University.

Farley, Reynolds. 1977. "Trends in Racial Inequalities: Have the Gains of the 1960s Disappeared in the 1970s?" *American Sociological Review* 42 (April): 189–208.

———. 1984. *Blacks and Whites: Narrowing the Gap?* Cambridge: Harvard University Press.

Farley, Reynolds, and Walter R. Allen. 1987. *The Color Line and the Quality of Life in America.* New York: Russell Sage.

Farley, Reynolds, and Suzanne M. Bianchi. 1983. "The Growing Gap between Blacks." *American Demographics,* July, 15–18.

Feagin, Joe R., and Melvin P. Sikes. 1994. *Living with Racism: The Black Middle-Class Experience.* Boston: Beacon.

Featherman, David, and Robert Hauser. 1976. "Changes in the Socioeconomic Stratification of Races, 1962–1973." *American Journal of Sociology* 82 (November): 621–651.

Fernandez, John. 1981. *Racism and Sexism in Corporate Life: Changing Values in American Business.* Lexington, Mass.: Lexington Books.

Flanagan, Robert J. 1976. "Actual versus Potential Impact of Government Anti-Discriminating Programs." *Industrial and Labor Relations Review* 29 (July): 486–507.

Fortune. 1968. "The Editor's Desk." January, 127–128.

Franklin, Raymond S., and Solomon Resnik. 1973. *The Political Economy of Racism.* New York: Holt.

Frazier, E. Franklin. 1957. *The Black Bourgeoisie: The Rise of a New Middle Class.* New York: Free Press.

Freeman, Richard. 1973. "Changes in the Labor Market for Black Americans, 1968–1972." *Brookings Papers on Economic Activity 1* (Summer): 57–120.

———. 1976a. *The Black Elite.* New York: McGraw-Hill.

———. 1976b. *The Over-Educated American.* New York. Academic Press.

———. 1981. "Black Economic Progress after 1964: Who Has Gained and Why." In *Studies in Labor Markets,* ed. S. Rosen, 247–295. Chicago: University of Chicago Press.

Fromm, Erich. 1955. *The Sane Society.* New York: Rinehart, Mills.

Gershman, Carl, and Kenneth Clark. 1980. "A Matter of Class." *New York Times Magazine,* October 5, 22.

Gibson, Parke D. 1978. *$70 Billion in the Black: America's Black Consumers.* New York: Macmillan.

Glasgow, Douglas G. 1980. *The Black Underclass: Poverty, Unemployment, and Entrapment of Ghetto Youth.* San Francisco: Jossey-Bass.

Hampton, Robert E. 1977. "The Response of Governments and the Civil Service to Antidiscrimination Efforts." In *Equal Rights and Industrial Relations,* ed. L. Hausman, O. Ashenfelter, B. Rustin, R. F. Schubert, and D. Slaiman. Madison, Wis.: Industrial Relations Research Association.

Harrington, Alan. 1959. *Life in the Crystal Palace.* New York: Knopf.

Harrington, Michael. 1984. *The New American Poverty.* New York: Holt, Rinehart, and Winston.

Harris, Ron. 1994. "The Riots Helped No One — Except the Well-Placed Few." *Los Angeles Times,* 1 May, sec. B, 1.

Hauser, Robert, and David Featherman. 1974. "White/Non-White Differentials in Occupational Mobility among Men in the United States, 1962–1972." *Demography* 11: 247–266.

Hausman, Leonard, Orley Ashenfelter, Bayard Rustin, Richard F. Schubert, and Donald Slaiman, eds. 1977. *Equal Rights and Industrial Relations.* Madison, Wis.: Industrial Relations Research Association.

Haworth, Joan, James Gwartney, and Charles Haworth. 1975. "Earnings, Productivity, and Changes in Employment Discrimination during the 1960s." *American Economic Review* 65 (March): 158–168.

Haynes, Ulric, Jr. 1968. "Equal Job Opportunity: The Credibility Gap." *Harvard Business Review,* May–June, 113–120.

Heckman, James J. 1976. "Simultaneous Equation Models with and without Structural Shifts in Equations." In *Studies in Non-linear Estimation,* ed. Stephen Goldfeld and Richard Quandt, 235–272. Cambridge, Mass.: Ballinger.

Heckman, James J., and Brook S. Payner. 1989. "Determining the Impact of Federal Antidiscrimination Policy on the Economic Status of Blacks: A Study of South Carolina." *American Economic Review* 79: 138–177.

Heckman, James J., and Kenneth Wolpin. 1976. "Does the Contract Compliance Program Work? An Analysis of Chicago Data." *Industrial and Labor Relations Review* 29 (July).

Heidrick and Struggles, Inc. 1979a. *Chief Personnel Executives Look at Blacks in Business.* Chicago: Heidrick and Struggles.

———. 1979b. *Profile of a Black Executive.* Chicago: Heidrick and Struggles.

Henderson, Hazel. 1968. "Should Business Tackle Society's Problem?" *Harvard Business Review,* July–August, 77–82.

Herring, Cedric, and Sharon Collins. 1995. "Retreat from Equal Opportunity? The Case of Affirmative Action." In *The Bubbling Cauldron,* ed. J. Feagin. Minneapolis: University of Minnesota Press.

Hertz, Diane. 1990. "Worker Displacement in a Period of Rapid Job Expansion: 1983–87." *Monthly Labor Review* (Bureau of Labor Statistics), May, 21–33.

Hill, Herbert. 1977. "The Equal Employment Acts of 1964 and 1972: A Critical Analysis of the Legislative History and Administration of the Law." *Industrial Relations Law Journal* 2, 1 (Spring): 1–98.

Hout, Michael. 1984. Occupational Mobility of Black Men: 1962–1973. American Sociological Review 49: 308–322.

Hudson, William, and Walter Broadnax. 1982. "Equal Employment Opportunity: A Public Policy." *Public Personnel Management* 11: 268–276.

Isaac, Larry, and William R. Kelly. 1981. "Racial Insurgency, the State, and Welfare Expansion: Local and National Level Evidence from the Postwar United States. *American Journal of Society* 6 (May): 1348–1385.

Ismail, Sherille. 1985. "Despite Gains of the 1960s and 1970s Blacks' Progress Lags Behind Whites'." Pp. 10–12 in *Point of View* 20 (Spring/Summer). Washington, D.C.: Congressional Black Caucus Foundation Inc.

Jackall, Robert. 1988. *Moral Mazes: The World of Corporate Managers.* Oxford: Oxford University Press.

Jackson, Jesse L. 1979. *Straight from the Heart.* Philadelphia: Fortress Press.

Jaynes, Gerald David, and Robin M. Williams, Jr. 1989. *A Common Destiny: Blacks and American Society.* Washington, D.C.: National Academy Press.

Jones, Edward W. 1986. "Black Managers: The Dream Deferred." *Harvard Business Review,* May–June, 84–89.

Kanter, Rosabeth. 1977. *Men and Women of the Corporation.* New York: Basic Books.

Kasarda, John D. 1980. "The Implications of Contemporary Redistribution Trends for National Policy." *Social Science Quarterly* 61: 373–400.

———. 1986. "The Regional and Urban Redistribution of People and Jobs in the U.S." Working paper prepared for the National Research Council Committee on National Urban Policy, National Academy of Sciences.

Kirschenman, Jolene, and Kathryn M. Neckerman. 1991. " 'We'd Love to

Hire Them, But . . .': The Meaning of Race for Employers." In *The Urban Underclass*, ed. C. Jencks and P. Peterson, 203–232. Washington, D.C.: Brookings.

Korn/Ferry. 1986. *Korn/Ferry International's Executive Profile: A Survey of Corporate Leaders in the Eighties*. New York: Korn/Ferry. Pamphlet.

———. 1990. *Korn/Ferry International's Executive Profile: A Decade of Changes in Corporate Leadership*. New York: Korn/Ferry. Pamphlet.

Landry, Bart. 1987. *The New Black Middle Class*. Berkeley: University of California Press.

Lazaar, Edward. 1991. "Discrimination in Labor Markets." In *Essays on the Economics of Discrimination*, ed. E. Hoffman. Mich.: Upjohn Institute for Employment Research.

Leonard, Jonathan S. 1982. "The Impact of Affirmative Action on Minority and Female Employment." Working paper, School of Business Administration, University of California, Berkeley.

———. 1984. "The Impact of Affirmative Action on Employment." *Journal of Labor Economics* 2: 439–64.

———. 1988. "Women and Affirmative Action in the 1980s." Paper presented at the American Economic Association Annual Meeting, October.

Levitan, Sar. 1969. *The Great Society's Poor Law: A New Approach to Poverty*. Baltimore: Johns Hopkins University Press.

Levitan, Sar, William B. Johnson, and Robert Taggart. 1975. *Still a Dream: The Changing Status of Blacks since 1960*. Cambridge: Harvard University Press.

Loury, Glenn C. 1985. "The Moral Quandary of the Black Community." *Public Interest* 79 (Spring): 9–22.

Lydenberg, Steven D., Alice Tepper Marlin, Sean O'Brien Strub, and the Council on Economic Priorities. 1986. *Rating America's Corporate Conscience: A Provocative Guide to the Companies behind the Products You Buy Every Day*. Reading, Mass.: Addison-Wesley.

Maccoby, Michael. 1976. *The Gamesman*. New York: Simon and Schuster.

Marable, Manning. 1983. *How Capitalism Underdeveloped Black America: Problems of Race, Political Economy, and Society*. Boston: South End Press.

Mare, Robert D., and Christopher Winship. 1980. "Family Background, Race, and Youth Unemployment, 1968–1978: Evidence for a Black Underclass." Paper presented at the meetings of the American Sociological Association, New York, August.

Massey, Douglas S., and Nancy A. Denton. 1993. *American Apartheid: Segregation and the Making of the Underclass.* Cambridge: Harvard University Press.

McKersie, Robert. n.d. *Minority Employment Patterns in an Urban Labor Market: The Chicago Experience.* Report Commission of the Equal Employment Opportunity Commission. Washington, D.C.: Equal Employment Opportunity Commission.

Meier, August. 1967. "Civil Rights Strategies for Negro Employment." In *Employment, Race, and Poverty,* ed. A. M. Ross and Herbert Hill, 186–188. New York: Harcourt, Brace, and World.

Mills, Charles. 1951. *White Collar: The American Middle Classes.* New York: Oxford University Press.

Murray, Charles. 1984. *Losing Ground: American Social Policy, 1950–1980.* New York: Basic Books.

Nathan, Richard P. 1969. *Jobs and Civil Rights: The Role of the Federal Government in Promoting Equal Opportunity in Employment and Training.* Prepared for the U.S. Commission on Civil Rights. Washington, D.C.: Brookings.

Newman, Dorothy K., Nancy J. Amidei, Barbara L. Carter, Dawn Day, William J. Kruvant, and Jack S. Russell. 1978. *Protest, Politics, and Prosperity: Black Americans and White Institutions, 1940–1975.* New York: Pantheon.

Orfield, Gary, and Carol Ashkinaze. 1991. *The Closing Door: Conservative Policy and Black Opportunity.* Chicago: University of Chicago Press.

Ornati, Oscar A., and Anthony Pisano. 1972. "Affirmative Action: Why It Isn't Working." *Personnel Administration* 35 (September): 50–52.

Parsons, Donald O. 1980. "Racial Trends in Male Labor Force Participation." *American Economic Review* 70 (December): 911–920.

Peters, Tom. 1988. *Thriving on Chaos: Handbook for a Management Revolution.* New York: Knopf.

Pfeffer, Jeffrey. 1982. *Power in Organizations.* Boston: Pitman.

Piven, Frances Fox, and R. A. Cloward. 1971. *Regulating the Poor: The Functions of Public Welfare.* New York: Pantheon.

———. 1977. *Poor People's Movements: Why They Succeed, How They Fail.* New York: Pantheon.

Poole, Isiah. 1981. "Uncle Sam's Pink Slip." *Black Enterprise* 12 (December): 52.

Purcell, Theodore V. 1977. "Management and Affirmative Action in the Late Seventies." In *Equal Rights and Industrial Relations,* ed. L. Hausman, O. Ashenfelter, B. Rustin, R. F. Schubert, and D. Slaiman, 71–103. Madison, Wis.: Industrial Relations Research Association.

Ramos, Dante. 1994. "White Minorities." *New Republic,* 17 October, 24.

Reynolds, William B. 1983. "The Justice Department's Enforcement of Title VII." *Labor Law Journal* 34: 259–265.

Riesman, David, Nathan Glazer, and Reuel Denney. 1953. *The Lonely Crowd: A Study of the Changing American Character.* New York: Doubleday.

Ross, Heather L., and Isabel Sawhill. 1975. *Time of Transition: The Growth of Families Headed by Women.* Washington, D.C.: Urban Institute Press.

Sheppard, Harold L., and Herbert E. Stringer. 1966. *Civil Rights, Employment, and the Social Status of American Negroes.* Based on a report for the U.S. Commission on Civil Rights (contract no. CCR-66-5). Kalamazoo, Mich.: Upjohn Institute for Employment Research.

Siegel, Paul M. 1965. "On the Cost of Being Negro." *Sociological Inquiry* 35 (Winter): 41–57.

Sitkoff, Harvard. 1978. *A New Deal for Blacks: The Emergence of Civil Rights as a National Issue.* New York: Oxford University Press.

——. 1981. *The Struggle for Black Equality: 1954–1980.* New York: Hill and Wang.

Smith, James P., and Finis R. Welch. 1977. "Black-White Male Wage Ratios, 1960–1970." *American Economic Review* 67 (June): 323–338.

——. 1978a. *The Convergence to Racial Equality in Women's Wages.* Santa Monica, Calif.: Rand Corporation.

——. 1978b. *Race Differences in Earnings: A Survey and New Evidence.* Santa Monica, Calif.: Rand Corporation.

——. 1983. "Longer Trends in Black/White Economic Status and Recent Effects of Affirmative Action." Paper presented at the Social Science Research Council Conference, Chicago.

——. 1984. "Affirmative Action and Labor Markets." *Journal of Labor Economics* 2: 269–299.

——. 1986. *Closing the Gap: Forty Years of Economic Progress for Blacks.* Santa Monica, Calif.: Rand Corporation.

Sowell, Thomas. 1983. "The Economics and Politics of Race." *Firing Line,* November. Transcript.

Starobin, Paul. 1993. "Unequal Shoes." *National Journal,* 11 September, 2176–2179.

Theodore, Nikolas C., and D. Garth Taylor. 1991. *The Geography of Op-*

portunity: The Status of African Americans in the Chicago Area Economy. Chicago: Chicago Urban League.

Thurow, Lester. 1969. *Poverty and Discrimination.* Washington, D.C.: Brookings.

Urban League. 1961. *Equal Rights — Greater Responsibility: The Challenge to Community Leadership in 1961.* Chicago: Urban League.

U.S. Bureau of the Census. 1963. *Occupational Characteristics.* Series PC(2)-7A. Washington, D.C.: Bureau of the Census.

———. 1973. *Occupational Characteristics.* Series PC(2)-7A. Washington, D.C.: Bureau of the Census.

———. 1979a. *Social and Economic Status of the Black Population in the United States, 1790–1978: A Historical View.* Series P-23, no. 80. Washington, D.C.: Bureau of the Census.

———. 1979b. *1977 Survey of Minority-Owned Business Enterprises: Black.* Series MB77-1. Washington, D.C.: Social and Economic Statistics Administration.

———. 1980a. *Characteristics of the Population: Detailed Population Characteristics.* pt. 1, sec. A. Series PC-80-1-D1-A. Washington, D.C.: Bureau of the Census.

———. 1980b. *Current Population Reports: Money and Income of Persons in 1979.* Series P-60, no. 129. Washington, D.C.: Bureau of the Census.

———. 1982. *1982 Survey of Minority-Owned Business Enterprises: Black.* Series MB82-1. Washington, D.C.: Bureau of the Census.

U.S. Bureau of Labor Statistics. 1982. *Current Population Survey: 1983 Annual Averages. Basic Table.* Washington, D.C.: Bureau of Labor Statistics.

———. n.d. Office of Employment and Statistics tables. Washington, D.C.: Bureau of Labor Statistics.

U.S. Commission on Civil Rights. 1969. *Staff Memorandum.* February 4. Washington, D.C.: U.S. Government Printing Office.

U.S. Department of Commerce. 1979. *A Strategy for Minority Business Enterprise Development.* Washington, D.C.: Minority Business Development Agency.

———. 1980. *1978 Status of Minorities and Women in State and Local Governments.* Washington, D.C.: Equal Employment Opportunity Commission.

———. 1981a. *Minority Business Development in the Eighties.* Washington, D.C.: Minority Business Development Agency.

———. 1981b. *Performance for Minority Business Development, Fiscal Year 1980.* Washington, D.C.: Minority Business Development Agency.

U.S. Department of Housing and Urban Development. 1991. *Housing Discrimination Study.* Washington, D.C.: U.S. Government Printing Office.

U.S. Equal Employment Opportunity Commission. 1978. *Ninth Annual Report.* Washington, D.C.: U.S. Government Printing Office.

———. 1980a. *1978 Status of Minorities and Women in State and Local Governments.* Washington, D.C.: Equal Employment Opportunity Commission.

———. 1980b. *Federal Civilian Work Force Statistics.* AR-80-21 (November). Washington, D.C.: Office of Personnel Management.

———. 1982. *Job Patterns for Minorities and Women in Private Industry.* Vol. 1. Washington, D.C.: U.S. Government Printing Office.

———. n.d. Report. Washington, D.C.: Office of Program Research, Survey Division.

U.S. Kerner Commission. 1968. *Report of the National Advisory Commission on Civil Disorders.* New York: Bantam.

U.S. Senate Committee on Labor and Public Welfare, Subcommittee on Civil Rights. 1954. *Antidiscrimination in Employment: Hearings 5.692.* 23–25 February, 1–3 March.

Vroman, Wane. 1974. "Changes in Black Workers' Relative Earnings: Evidence from the 1960s." In *Patterns of Racial Discrimination,* ed. George M. Furstenbery, Bennett Harrison, and Ann Horowitz. Lexington, Mass.: Heath.

Wall Street Journal. 1984. "Taking a Chance: Many Blacks Jump off the Corporate Ladder to be Entrepreneurs." 2 August, sec. 1, 1.

———. 1988. "Labor Letter: A Special News Report on People and Their Jobs in Offices, Fields, and Factories." 9 February, 1.

White, Theodore. 1964. *The Making of the President.* New York: Atheneum.

Whittingham-Barnes, Donna. 1993. "Workforce Trends: Is There Life after Unemployment?" *Black Enterprise,* February, 181–186.

Whyte, William H., Jr. 1956. *The Organization Man.* New York: Simon and Schuster.

Williams, Walter. 1982. "Rethinking the Black Agenda." In *Proceedings of the Black Alternatives Conference,* 16–31. San Diego, Calif.: New Coalition for Economic and Social Change.

Wilson, Cynthia A., James H. Lewis, and Cedric Herring. 1991. *The 1991 Civil Rights Act: Restoring Our Basic Protections.* Chicago: Chicago

Urban League and Chicago Lawyers' Committee for Civil Rights under Law.

Wilson, William J. 1978. *The Declining Significance of Race*. Chicago: University of Chicago Press.

———. 1981. "The Black Community in the 1980s: Questions of Race, Class, and Public Policy." *Annals of the American Academy of Political and Social Sciences* 454: 26–41.

———. 1984. *Race, Economics, and Corporate America*. Wilmington, Del.: Scholarly Resources.

———. 1987. *The Truly Disadvantaged: The Inner City, the Underclass, and Public Policy*. Chicago: University of Chicago Press.

Wolkinson, Benjamin W. 1973. *Black Unions and the EEOC*. Lexington, Mass.: Heath.

Yarmolinsky, A. 1969. "The Beginning of OEO." In *On Fighting Poverty: Perspectives from Experience,* ed. James L. Sundquist, 34–51. New York: Basic Books.

Zweigenhaft, Richard L., and G. William Domhoff. 1991. *Blacks in the White Establishment? A Study of Race and Class in America*. New Haven: Yale University Press.

INDEX

accounting: affirmative action programs in, 61; blacks underrepresented in, 50; racialization of jobs in, 38–42

advertising firms, black-owned, racialization of jobs in, 38–42

affirmative action: black CEOs in, 73–75, 147–151, 172n.5; black economic opportunity and, 17–27, 118, 158–159; black groups' pressure for, 107–111; career-enhancing strategies and, 81–84; challenges to, xi–xii, 17, 169n.1 (Chapter 2); compliance with anti-discrimination legislation through, 100–107; downsizing and flattening of corporations and, 144–147; economic conditions and, 166–168; education levels and, 9–10; expansion of, 18–19; federal contract compliance and, 20–21, 60–63; fragility of African American middle class and, 162–168; individual and group activism of black executives and, 90–93, 104–105; job security issues facing, 126–129; legal challenges to, 119–120, 170nn.1–2; mainstreaming of black executives and, 73–75, 85–89; as mobility trap for black executives, 77–80, 102–107; racial equality and, 159–161; racialized jobs and, 77–80, 157–159

African American business elite. *See* black corporate executives

African American–owned business sector, racialized roles in, 37–42

Aid to Families with Dependent Children, 24; racialized jobs for African Americans in, 31

Allen, Walter R., 17

Althauser, Robert, 25

American Can Company, 59

American Telephone and Telegraph (AT&T), EEOC charges against, 19

Anderton, Douglas L., 146

Anheuser-Busch, 128–129

Arthur Andersen & Company, 61

Ashenfelter, Orley, 20–21, 60

Ashkinaze, Carol, 145

Bakke, Allan, 119–120

Barrett, Richard E., 146

Bay Area Rapid Transit system (BART), 60

"beached" executives, 150, 152

Becker, Brian, 6–7

black corporate executives: career-enhancing strategies of, 81–89, 129–133; defined, 13; downsizing and flattening of job market for, 144–147; elite status of, xi–xiii; exiting executives, characteristics of, 133–136; external relations with black groups, 107–111; golden handcuffs for, 93–96; history of hiring practices for, 45–48, 116–118; individual and group activism of, 90–93, 102–107;